Rescued and Redeemed

Cockroach No More

How God helped me to overcome
my feelings of shame and regret
when my husband
committed the Unspeakable

JEANNIE LAVERNE

WESTBOW®
PRESS
A DIVISION OF THOMAS NELSON
& ZONDERVAN

WestBow Press books may be ordered through
booksellers or by contacting:

WestBow Press
A Division of Thomas Nelson & Zondervan
1663 Liberty Drive
Bloomington, IN 47403
www.westbowpress.com
1-(866) 928-1240

ISBN: 978-1-4908-0695-2 (sc)
ISBN: 978-1-4908-0697-6 (hc)
ISBN: 978-1-4908-0696-9 (e)

Library of Congress Control Number: 2013915816

Printed in the United States of America.

WestBow Press rev. date: 03/10/2014

This book is dedicated to all the moms of abused children. You are all over-comers.

I am like a cockroach.
Like an untouchable,
Smelly, black creature
That crawls through the darkness,
Running for its life.
No one wants to look at me.
No one wants to acknowledge my existence.
If they were to step on me
The smell would be too great.
I cannot be in the same place as ordinary humans,
For it would make them uncomfortable.
They cannot be around what they don't understand.
My shame is unbearable.
My ex-husband molested my daughter
When she was five years old.
Here is my story.

May 1991:
The Admission

It was storming. The lightning lit up the sky. The rumbling of the thunder matched the churning of my insides. We had just come home from another counseling session for Jozie. My six-year-old daughter was not talking much to the counselor. Why wouldn't she tell the counselor what she wanted to hear? Why wouldn't Jozie tell the counselor who had molested her?

I was in the kitchen pondering this when Jozie walked in, her hazel eyes big and round, fear showing like I've seen before. She hated storms, and so did I. I gave her a comforting hug, and we sat down to supper. I had picked up some ribs on the way home, and they tasted good. While we were eating our ribs, I got the feeling that Jozie was ready to talk but needed someone either to ask the right questions or to say it for her so she could agree with them.

In the car on the way home, Jozie had asked me if I liked Daddy, and I told her that I used to but not anymore, not after I found out that he hurt her.

She also said that she was really mad at him, so I told her that it was okay to be angry at him. After a little while, we passed a police cruiser, and Jozie called my attention to it. I told her that cops were nothing to be afraid of and asked her who told her to be afraid of cops. Her dad, she had answered. I told her that he was lying to her.

I had sat in on the counseling session again and was tired of the way they were going. Puppets, books, stories, and more puppets. Hadn't Jozie already told her kindergarten teacher and the employees at her day care what had happened and who did it? Were all the people who were supposedly helping us dense?

I took the plunge and asked the big question. "Jozie, did your daddy say that he would shoot me if you told that he hurt you?"

She said, "Yes. He told me that on my birthday."

"Is that why you shouted out that you wouldn't tell?" I asked.

"Yes," she answered.

We finished eating, and Jozie went to the living room to watch television. I had to clean up Danny, her one-year-old brother, and do dishes.

After I was done in the kitchen, I sat down on the other end of the couch from Jozie and asked, "Can I ask you some more questions about Daddy hurting you? You've already told me a lot. I would like to know everything."

"No," she answered.

"Please."

Jozie looked at me but didn't say anything.

"Where in this house did Daddy hurt you?" I asked.

"In my bed."

"Did he hurt you when I was at home or when I was gone to church choir practice?"

"At night when I was sleeping."

"What did he say when he came into your bedroom?"

"He said, 'I'm coming in for a visit.'"

With all the self-control I could muster, I asked her, "What part of his body did he hurt you with?"

"His penis," she answered.

I got up and walked into the kitchen. I did not cry, but anger consumed me. How could the father of my child be such a monster? I was hoping and praying that I had caught it early and that he had only done it for one summer.

I had to ask a few more questions to find out, so I walked back to the living room, sat down with Jozie, and asked, "Why didn't you call out to me so that I could make him stop hurting you?"

"He said he would spank me if I said anything."

"Did Daddy hurt you when I was at choir practice?"

"Yes, only once."

"Was it hot outside when he hurt you?"

"Yes."

"Did Daddy hurt you while Danny was in Mommy's tummy?"

"No."

"Did Daddy hurt you before Mommy's tummy stuck out with Danny?"

3

"No."

"Did Daddy hurt you after Danny came out of Mommy's tummy?"

"Yes."

So, I was pretty sure that it only happened for one summer after all. I wanted to cry, but instead I told Jozie how glad I was that she told me these things, and that it must have been very hard for her to do. I asked her if I could give her a hug, and she climbed into my arms. Danny toddled over to us, and we all hugged. I gave a weak smile and told Jozie how brave she was.

November 1989:
The Affair

I guess it all started when the man I had been married to for ten years sat me down on the living room couch two days before Thanksgiving in 1989 and told me that he was having an affair. I don't recall being terribly shocked, because his behavior had been suspicious long before then. While I was pregnant with his son, he had traveled to Las Vegas and Maryland for short "vacations" and left me behind. He was gone at night "working late" or "going to the movies" with no ticket stub in his pocket on laundry day. He had joined a popular dieting program and lost nearly forty pounds. Loneliness consumed me, and instead of a healthy diet for my baby's sake, I ate peanut M&Ms every chance I got.

Danny had been born earlier that year, in August. My water broke early in the morning at home, so we went to the hospital. I had almost no labor pains at all. The doctors found that he was breech, so a C-section was performed. Danny came out small but healthy. He had a red patch on his forehead that the doctor said he would outgrow. I thought he looked wonderful, but my husband said that he was the ugliest baby he had ever seen. Now, looking back on that day, I realize why my husband said that. Danny, my only son, looked just like me.

However, I digress. I still went to the family dinners on that Thanksgiving back in 1989, not letting on that anything was wrong. We had dinners on both sides of the family to attend. I was panicking inside and wondering how to feel. I was angry, sad, and desperately lonely. I wanted to save our marriage. I had invested over ten years in it. I also knew that I did not want to go home to my own family as a failure. I was afraid to face them. Little did I know that my situation was soon to get much worse.

The affair did not end. My soon-to-be ex would still come home late. Christmas that year was especially stressful, and my poor daughter could feel the tension. On Christmas morning, with each gift that she opened, she cried out, "Oh, this is just what I wanted!" She shouted this over and over. She was four years old, and, at the time, it was cute, but now I'm sure she was stressed.

The tension, the affair, and my loneliness continued. One morning in January 1990, he arrived at home just as I was awakening to get ready for work. I threw a suitcase at him and told him that I wanted him gone when I got home from work. He moved out of our house and into his girlfriend's apartment.

I was alone, utterly alone, for the first time in my life. At night, after the kids were in bed, I would sit on the couch, frozen, just staring at the television. I don't think that I cared what was on. I just stared. Although the kids slept through the night, I could not sleep. I wanted my husband back. I wanted to be happily married. I started marriage counseling on my own to try to "fix" myself so that my marriage would work. I went to a new church. I went to work. I took care of the kids. The loneliness was ever-present. January and February dragged by.

He would still call me. He even told me his new address. I tried to think of ways to get him back. In March, on Easter morning, I dressed everybody up and drove to his apartment, hoping to invite him to church with us. He was not home. Another time, I visited him at a bar, where I knew he would be shooting pool with his buddies. He went home to the other woman that night. We would have lunch together and end up yelling.

On April 4, we had one of those lunches, and I wrote some of the things he said in my journal. He said that he didn't like children; he felt guilty; he wouldn't abandon me; he wanted to leave both women and live as a hermit; he missed his freedom and wanted to pick up and go. These comments made sense to me much later.

A couple of weeks after that, he invited me to a work-related dinner. I dressed up, fixed my hair, painted my nails, found a baby-sitter, and drove to his apartment to meet him. I was invited into his apartment while he was finishing fixing his tie. I saw a picture of 'her' and some of his belongings and, after using their bathroom, had noticed that he had picked up our beautiful, velvety, blue bedspread from the drycleaners and put it on their bed. No wonder the clerk could not find it when I went to pick it up a couple of weeks earlier. I was angry. He was starting a new life without me, taking our things without telling me, and by agreeing to go to this dinner, I felt like a pawn in a chess game. He was just using me for appearances sake. In the car as he drove to the dinner, angry words flew. I hit him on his shoulder, and then he hit me. Then I let him have it with my purse. He told me never to do that again. After some more arguing, we both calmed down, and the rest of the car ride was uneventful.

The dinner at the country club was magnificent. We got through the delicious meal, and then went to the outside deck to talk. I did some fancy apologizing and talking. We hugged. There was even a shooting star on that clear, cool night. However, in the back of my mind, I knew it was over. His demeanor was one of apology, but I could tell he wanted out of the marriage. After the dinner, our living situations did not change.

Being the stubborn person I was, I gave him an ultimatum. Come home and stop having the affair, or I would file for divorce. On May 9, 1990, I went to an attorney that a friend recommended and filed for separation and provisional relief. A hearing was set for May 14. He came home then, but he didn't bring all his belongings. The provisional relief was postponed. I suggested marriage counseling, and he begrudgingly agreed. We went to the holistic counselor I had already been seeing, and the usual questions were asked and answered. He seemed quite nervous and guarded in his answers. When the counselor brought up 'her,' I recall noticing that his face actually changed. His eyes lit up a bit and his face softened. My heart sank a bit, but I wanted to try and save our marriage. So, I tried to overlook this and focus on us.

I really liked the counselor. She was supportive and listened to us; I felt that she could help us. My husband was not so enthusiastic; he stopped going to counseling after a few sessions. I, on the other hand, continued for several months, thankful for someone to talk to. Looking back, I now can see that she knew the marriage would be ending. But she was always there for me, encouraging me and helping me through. She is the one who encouraged me to journal my feelings and what was going on in my life.

June 1990:
Make or Break

I tried. I *really* tried. I was the perfect wife. I cooked, cleaned, smiled, did the laundry, and worked very hard to please him.

Meanwhile, he took a vacation by himself. He stayed out late, shooting pool with his buddies. He took motorcycle rides by himself. He watched X-rated movies. He ignored the children. He spent a tremendous amount of money. I explained to him that the expenditures bothered me, and he said that I should have told him sooner, so that there would be more money for him. He wouldn't respond to my sexual advances. I would ask him why he came home and why he was at the house, and he never had a good answer. He also made me feel bad every time I wanted to go somewhere without the children.

I joined the church choir in July, and there was no babysitting during the Thursday-night rehearsals. So I asked him to babysit for me. He agreed. Our relationship seemed to improve a little. And I was so happy to be singing again. July was a good month. Then August arrived and something was amiss at our house. Jozie started displaying strange behavior. She didn't want to be left at home without me.

One Thursday I came home from choir practice, and she came running out of the house to me. We went back into the house together, and I found my husband lying on the couch in the living room with a blanket on, playing with his genitals. There was a movie on the TV, and Danny was sitting on the floor. Both children were fully clothed, so I didn't even begin to read any more into his actions. I scolded him fiercely, and Jozie and I went to the grocery.

I had no idea that he was molesting Jozie. I had not been educated about that type of thing and did not recognize the signs. I look back at this moment and wish I had taken her to the police that very night. She may have told the authorities what had happened, and my ex would have gone to jail. She was only five years old, and I was ignorant.

September-October 1990: Shock and Fear

School was back in session, so it was back to work for me. One day I mentioned to a trusted colleague at work that my family was acting weird and things just weren't right at home. She gave me a pamphlet on sexual abuse, and I was shocked. She also recommended a counseling center, which I talked my husband into going to. The counselor suggested a six-week time frame for our counseling, and we both agreed to go.

The first counseling session went without incident. I tried to recall all that had been going on during the entire marriage. I remembered overnight visits to his parents' house; we had spent the night because it was a five-hour drive from our home. His mom had always been exhausted the next day. I also talked about how Jozie had been displaying odd behavior: riding one of her teddy bears in a sexual way.

I'm sure that I was in denial that my husband had done anything wrong. So in the second counseling session, on September 4, I admitted to the counselor that I thought his mom was molesting Jozie. I felt confused and upset, so much so that my head felt like it was spinning. But God was looking out for me and so was the counselor. Once I had expressed my feelings about his mom, the counselor suggested that we go out to eat at a public restaurant. We did. We had driven from work to the counseling session in our own cars. I went to go pick up the kids from day care, and he went to the restaurant.

During the dinner, he called his mother on a pay phone at the restaurant. I was at the table watching him, sitting with our two children. Of course, both he and his mom denied my concern and called me crazy. Luckily, he didn't say much at the table. I knew he was angry by the tone of his voice and the way he was acting. For the first time in my life, I feared for my safety. My husband was six feet tall and over two hundred pounds. And I had just accused his mother of sexual misconduct in front of a counselor. What was he going to do? He left the restaurant. I was relieved, but I had to go home by myself with the children. He went to stay with the other woman again.

The next morning at six, his sister rang my doorbell. She was loaded down with gifts for my children, and she said she wanted to take the children with her for a visit. I let her know that it was a school day. She wanted to come in then, but I did not let her. I told her I had to go to work and that it wasn't a good time. I remember her frowning at me and dropping the gifts on our front step with disgust. I also remember locking the deadbolt on the door as she left.

My anxiety level was high. I could not figure out what was going on. His whole family was acting weird. Why would his sister bring gifts and want to take the kids for a visit during the week? The only way that I got through any of this was the fact that God was watching out for me and my children. He had to have given me the strength and courage to say what I said and to do what I did. I had no idea how people act in situations like ours.

A few days later, on Saturday, September 8, I got a call from my husband in the evening. He let me know that he was upset with me and that he was coming over. I got a terrible feeling in the pit of my stomach. Why was he coming over? Was he going to try to take Jozie like his sister had? I put my son in his crib in his bedroom. I paced back and forth and prayed and prayed. An answer came: "Put Jozie in the shower." I was skeptical, but I started the shower and had Jozie get under the running water.

He had arrived on his motorcycle with a friend— some man he worked with, I guess. I don't recall the man's name or what he looked like. I let them in, and the man sat down on the couch in the living room. I was pretty sure that my husband had been drinking. He demanded to know where Jozie was, and I told him that she was in the shower. I argued with him and repeatedly tried to call the police. Each time I picked up the phone, though, he pressed the button to stop the call. I guess he decided it was time to get Jozie and go. We both were in the hallway, and

I put my hands out to the door frame to block his entrance to the bathroom. He slapped me on both sides of my face, but I did not fall. I did not waver; I stood my ground. The man in the living room reacted with a gasp. My husband backed away from me and went to the basement for something. I took that opportunity to call the cops. When he came up from the basement, he was fumbling with something in his pocket. The police arrived just as he entered the living room. They asked me if I was all right. I touched my cheeks and said I was. They asked my husband to leave. He did, taking that other man with him. I shut and locked the door tight, got Jozie out of the shower, and put her to bed. I had a headache and my cheeks hurt. I looked in the mirror and saw no bruising or swelling. Then I called a friend, who recommended that I go to a women's shelter in town. I took some acetaminophen and went to bed.

The next day, September 9, after confiding in a friend, I packed up my children and went to the women's shelter she recommended. The room we stayed in had only bunk beds for Jozie and me with a crib for my son. It was a dreary, lonely room. The shelter had rules and regulations, and I had to do a list of chores to get a free meal for my children and me. I did go to one counseling session there and received more information about abusive husbands. The next morning I looked at the list of chores and at the food on the stove and decided that I had a house of my own to take care of. I didn't need double chores. So we left the shelter, bought some fast food, and went home.

But I still needed to protect my children and myself. I took the next day off from work to let my cheeks and my pride heal. I was afraid to take Jozie to school for fear that my husband might show up and take her. I called my counselor, and she recommended that I change my locks and file a restraining order. So I did. I even changed the security code on our house alarm. I also had to let the school and the day care know that I was the only person to be picking up my children. I also filed for separation and provisional relief again on September 11, 1990. My legal records show that we had a court date on September 28 to set up the provisional relief and to make the restraining order reciprocal.

Those days were extremely difficult for me. I was frightened for my safety, but I had to go to work. I had to protect my children. I was afraid to go to sleep, so I kept the bedroom light on all night. I would think back to the night that he came over and tried to take Jozie and fear and anger consumed me. I kept wondering what he had gone down to the basement for and what was he fumbling with in his pocket when the police had arrived. We had bought a hand gun about a year earlier and both of us had practiced shooting it. We kept it in a top drawer in a locked file cabinet in the basement. Had he brought the gun up from the basement that night? Was he going to use it on me? I'm not sure to this day, but when I packed up my house for the move in August, the gun was nowhere to be found.

I came home from work one day to find my bedroom window screen pulled out and lying in the backyard. Someone had gotten in and tried to turn off the alarm. I assumed it was my husband, and I was very glad that I had changed the alarm code. Nothing was missing from the house. I changed the alarm code again and carried some of my jewelry to school with me so that if anyone got into the house, it wouldn't be stolen.

I was advised to take Jozie to be checked for venereal diseases. We went to the medical center in town, where it was discovered that she had chlamydia, so she had to take antibiotics. We also had to talk to the local children services. I wanted to disappear; I was a teacher—what was I doing at children services? I was very angry and scared. They put me through their questioning and observation procedures. It appeared to them that I was perfectly normal. Well, go figure.

I found myself meeting with my attorney again, and this time I filed for dissolution of marriage. My records show that this happened on October 15. I knew I had to go through with it that time. I couldn't help thinking that if I had followed through with the divorce back in May, Jozie would not have been molested. I do not know for sure when the abuse started, and I will probably never know, because my ex still maintains his innocence. But I could have prevented it that summer, so I have had to do a lot of soul searching with God in this area.

Meanwhile, Jozie was in counseling, but the sessions were not productive. She was not talking about the abuse. Until then, I had only blamed my husband's mother for molesting her. But the hospital staff said that to get chlamydia, a person had to have sexual intercourse.

Both my husband and I were to get checked for venereal diseases. I was negative. He took quite a while to get checked, but his test came back negative also. My guess is that my husband's girlfriend, an exotic dancer, knew this and helped him take some antibiotics before his test. Back then, it was fairly easy to get them.

I still did not want to believe that my husband had molested my daughter. I couldn't believe it. I did, however, make sure that I was present at any and all visits Jozie had with her father during the next few months. My close friends and the counselor both suggested that a male figure in Jozie's life had to have caused her disease. They suggested that I never leave my children alone with my husband at any time. My journal notes list a Thanksgiving lunch and a Christmas visit with him, but nothing else. There may have been other visits, but I'm sure that I was present and that my husband never had the children alone again.

April 1991:
Double Confirmation

The next two months, January and February, were filled with work, cleaning house, protecting my children, and deciding if I wanted to prosecute my husband. I had no evidence except the venereal disease, to which he had proved negative. Jozie's counseling continued, Danny was growing, and I was an angry woman. My rage at my soon-to-be ex was like a silent beast waiting to pounce.

My sleepless nights continued and a depression set in. On March 13, as I was sitting in my classroom, I decided I'd had enough. The anger consumed me. I wanted to shout to the world what my husband had done. I felt like I couldn't breathe, and I got dizzy.

I managed to get to the next classroom and tell another teacher I was feeling poorly. She notified others, and they called an ambulance. They put heart monitors on me at the hospital, but after a while I was fine. They called it an 'anxiety attack', and the doctor suggested I take a few days off. But

I took only one day off. I had many 'anxiety attacks' after that one, but I was able to calm myself down so that I did not have to go to the hospital.

However, I was also suicidal. I wanted my pain to end. Every day was a struggle. Every waking moment was filled with silent rage at my husband. Every night, after I tucked the kids into bed, was filled with tears. I would think of killing my husband and then myself, but every time I did this, I would remind myself that my children needed me. I would tell myself that they needed me to be strong for them and to protect them from further harm. My personal counselor was very helpful during these terrible days.

On March 19, Jozie's sixth birthday, she invited several friends from school to go to a local pizza and game restaurant. I invited her dad since he hadn't tried anything for several months, it was a public place, and I didn't expect any trouble from him. (Looking back at this, I wonder why I invited him. Maybe I was hoping to confront him myself. Or, maybe I was subconsciously wanting a confession from him. I'm not really sure.)

We all sat down at the party table, which was in a different room from all the games and rides. I ordered the pizza, and Jozie opened her gifts. Then my husband showed up with his girlfriend, whom I had not invited. She wore high heels with a sweater and skirt. She reminded me of his mom. When the children went to play in the next room, my husband and his girlfriend followed them, and I followed a few minutes later. I think that I must have been arranging the gifts or something. When I got to the other room, my husband was with Jozie, helping her with a ride. As I got closer, I could see him leaning close to her, talking in her ear. She yelled loudly, "I promise I won't tell!" My husband looked at me and laughed a nervous laugh. I didn't let on that I had heard her, so that a confrontation would be avoided during her party. But, of course, I then stayed with Jozie for the rest of the party. My suspicions about my husband were only confirmed.

Life went on pretty much the same until I received a phone call on April 9 from Jozie's kindergarten teacher. At that time, each school in this particular state was showing a kid-level video on sexual abuse. It showed what good hugs and bad hugs were and places on your body that no one should touch. Jozie's teacher told me that, while watching the video, Jozie had sat on her lap, hidden her face, and put her hands over her eyes so that there were just slits to see through. She said that Jozie hadn't cried or said anything during the video. When the video was over, Jozie held the teacher's hand and said to her, "I had that problem too, but it was my father." My worst fears had been confirmed again.

As I hung up the phone, in my mind's eye I saw myself collapsing on the floor and rolling up in a ball and crying. Back in those days, there were no cell phones, and I had taken the phone call in the main office of the school where I worked. So, I walked out of the office, down the hall, and back to my classroom. I was in a daze; I felt like I was not walking or doing anything on my own. Someone or something was helping me. (Thank you, Lord.)

I received a confidentially written letter from Jozie's teacher the next day at school stating again what she had said on the phone the day before. As I read it, my heart broke into so many pieces I was sure it would never be fixed. I didn't even know what I was teaching the children. I found myself looking out the window while leading songs. I couldn't tell anyone. I couldn't face the children. I wanted to run away. I missed work one day a week; each time was the day after one of Jozie's counseling sessions.

All I told anyone who asked about my marriage ending was that my husband had an affair. That, at least, was true. I did not tell my family about the abuse. I could not. I blamed myself; after all, I was the one who had given him an ultimatum to come back last May. During that time period—from May to August of the previous year—the sexual abuse apparently had happened.

Thankfully, I did have a small circle of girlfriends who believed me, listened to me, and helped me. Through their guidance, I filed for restricted visitation against my husband with the divorce attorney. The motion for restricted visitation came through on April 15, with the court date set for April 30. My husband had to agree to "appropriate psychological examination and testing," and he would never legally have the children alone with him again. I recall talking with my attorney about prosecuting my husband for the abuse, but he was against putting a six-year-old on the witness stand. I agreed with him.

It was time to get the divorce finalized and run home and hide. True, I had supervised visitation in place, but remembering the night my husband had tried to take her, I didn't trust him or truly feel safe. His parents had also been calling, wanting to visit with Jozie, but I didn't trust them either. I told my attorney my plan, and he did not disagree. I left him a post office box number through which he could reach me; it was in a different town than where I had planned to live. On June 30, the paperwork was filed so that the divorce hearing would be set for August 8, 1991.

I had a lot to do in two months. I had to sell the house, find a new place in the next state to live, and protect myself and my children. I found a realtor and cleaned my house, getting it ready for sale. I arranged for a large moving truck five days after the divorce was final. By mid-July I had already been to the new state to find an apartment and had put a deposit on it. I was excited about the move. It would be a fresh start, and I would feel safer. I got permission from my husband to sell a few larger items. I put what was left of his belongings on the front lawn. This was no easy task. I had to haul his weights and weight bench up from the basement. I let my anger do the moving. Then, I left the house while he came and got them. I put an ad in the paper to sell some furniture and anything I did not want to take with me. I called my brother to see if he could help me on my moving day. He and his wife agreed to come and help.

August 1991: The Divorce

August 8, arrived, and I was both nervous and excited. The divorce was scheduled for nine that morning, so I got up early and took Jozie and Danny to a friend's house. I wore my favorite skirt to look nice for court.

When I got to the courthouse, I had to wait. The court had scheduled several cases in front of ours. I tried to stay away from my husband so I would not have to talk to him or his girlfriend. But as I walked to the restroom, his girlfriend decided to follow me. She wanted to talk to me about the alleged abuse, so I told her that he did it. She said she did not believe me, and she proceeded to blame the day care where Jozie stayed after school. She was so adamant that she got in my face and backed me into a corner. I told her the facts again, slid past her, went back to the hallway outside the courtroom door, and stood with my attorney. Thankfully, she kept her distance from me while I waited with him for the hearing to start.

We finally got to go in, and the hearing began. Through the settlement, I got the house and one car, and my ex got his motorcycle and the truck. Since I had already given him his belongings, we got to keep what we had. We received sole ownership of our retirement benefits. We split up the loans and debts according to each of our incomes. Child support was ordered, and we were to share in the expense of medical insurance for the children. I was given permanent custody of our two children, and the visitation rights of my ex would be determined at a later date. It was also written in the divorce decree that I could move out of state with the children. Looking back on this, I realize I had a wise attorney who had my best interests at heart, and I am eternally grateful to him.

The hearing ended, we signed the papers, and I literally ran out of the courtroom. It was on the second floor, so I ran down the spiral steps, looked up to the railing above, and saw my ex looking down at me. My mind was racing along with my steps. I smiled and said, "Ta! Ta!" and waved at him. I think he said good-bye, but I was moving so fast, I didn't care. I got outside and had to walk to my car, which was parked a couple of blocks away. After one block, I finally slowed down a bit and let myself breathe. I was free. I was elated.

August 1991:
My New Life

I had turned in my resignation at school, and on the last day, which was a teacher's day without students, I was packing up my teacher supplies in my second-story classroom. While packing, I played a tune from a 45 rpm record that my sister-in-law had sent to me about a month earlier. I played it loudly and over and over. Some of the words were "You think I'd crumble? You think I'd lay down and die? Oh, no, not I. I will survive..." At first I cried, but as I listened to it, my spirits lifted. In this particular school, we had no air-conditioning so my classroom windows were open, but I didn't care who heard it or if it bothered anyone. I needed to hear it so that I could believe in myself and my inner strength. My sister-in-law probably had no idea how helpful that song was to me.

Then I went home to do more packing. I had too much to pack in too little time. I was eager to move and get the kids registered for the new school year. I stayed up all hours of the night packing and cleaning. My brother and his wife drove the five-hour trip that weekend to help me with the move. I had everything packed except the kitchen, and it took most of the day to pack and load the truck.

One of Jozie's girlfriends came over to say good-bye. They hugged and said that they would write. I said good-bye to her mother and resumed packing.

My brother declined to drive the moving truck the five hours to our new apartment. Being so huge, the truck had a stick shift, and he didn't trust himself to drive it that far. I called the truck company, and they referred me to another company to ask for a driver. I was able to get someone, but they couldn't come until the next day. I am grateful for his assistance. He had a stick shift to drive with a mom, a toddler, a young girl, and a cat all sitting in the front seat. My brother drove my car, and his wife drove their car home.

It took most of the day to get to the new apartment. We had to stop every so often for bathroom breaks and a food break. Once we got there, the driver helped us to unload the truck. The apartment was on the second floor, and we all worked very hard. A boy from a neighboring apartment also helped us to unload.

At one point the police stopped by to tell us we were blocking the apartment driveway and we had to reposition the truck. I was about to object, because I couldn't see how it could be repositioned. This driver shushed me, was respectful to the police, and took care of moving the truck. Again, my thanks go out to this man.

After unloading, the only item left on the truck was the upright piano. I went to the apartment office and asked for help with it. The apartment manager knew some men who could help, so she called them and they showed up later that evening. After they carried my piano up the stairs and into the apartment, I tried to offer them some supper, but they refused and went on their way.

My driver drove the truck to where it needed to be returned, and I followed in my car. I then dropped him off at the bus depot in town, and he caught a bus back to his town. It was very late, I was exhausted, and sleep was in order. The two-bedroom apartment was nice. I put Jozie in the larger bedroom and Danny in the smaller one. After so many sleepless nights in my old house, I slept soundly on the lumpy pull-out couch in the living room.

I had moved to the new state without securing a new job, so I worked at a local restaurant for about a month. Then I signed up to substitute teach in mid-September. I also decided to attend the church where I had gone as a little girl. I wanted to see the sanctuary and look at the huge carpenter's cup displayed there. It was a sight to behold, though it was not as huge as I recalled. I was accepted into the church choir there and given solos to sing. My children liked their Sunday school classes. My family seemed to accept me back into the fold and did not ask about the divorce. All that I offered to them was that my ex had an affair. I had lived in another state for close to nine years and had grown apart from my sisters and brother. It was going to take some time to get to know everyone again.

I thought that I had arranged my finances well, but the accumulated debt was close to 9,600 dollars. Each time my ex was to take my name off an account, I had to do it myself or bug him to do it. As I searched my files, I found a receipt for a 599-dollar watch that he had charged on our credit card without me knowing. He probably bought it to impress his mistress.

I had also bought a different used car. In the settlement, I had been given the family car, which was actually my ex's mom's car. I wanted to be rid of it, so I got permission from my ex to sell it prior to the divorce. I traded it in for a newer used car, and somehow I had not made the payments on this new car while the divorce was going on. Since I had purchased it back in June, when we moved to the new state, I was two months behind in my payments already.

I received a phone call from the loan agency as a warning, but I wasn't able to mail a payment until the day before they were going to repossess the car. They came in the middle of the night to take the car. I went out the next day and thought someone had stolen it. I was given notice of the repossession and had to go to an attorney and file a Chapter 13 bankruptcy to get it back.

I called the bank where the loan was and begging for mercy, stated that I would make all the late payments up, but the bank would not budge. Luckily, I lived on a bus route, and I could get to the attorney that way. I remember standing on a corner in the dark, waiting for a bus ride home after papers were signed with the attorney. Danny was in my arms, and I was holding Jozie's hand. I was quite frightened standing there in that large town by myself. But we arrived home safely.

A friend that I had gone to high school with and who worked at the school where I was substituting drove me to work until I could get my car back. Once all the paperwork was filed, a neighbor that I had befriended drove us to the lot where the car was impounded. How wonderful is God with His blessings of friends!

Life was back to normal, and things were running smoothly. I was away from my ex; I was working almost every day; my children were healthy; and life was good. My ex didn't know exactly where I was, and my divorce attorney was not contacting me, so I thought all was well.

At night, after the kids were in bed, I found myself reminiscing about my childhood. Some of my memories were unpleasant but other memories I relished. I remembered the fun I had playing at my grandparents' farm. These days my grandparents were ill, living in a nursing home, and the farm had been sold. But I remembered their kindness and all the good food at their farmhouse. They had many cats at the farm, and the barn was a favorite place to play. We had a hayloft to climb in and a tire swing in a tree to swing on. There was a junkyard in the back where we had great fun finding things to play house with. And we played tag in one of their fields.

They had workhorses, but we weren't allowed to ride them.

I recalled one incident when I went out to the field with my grandpa to feed the cows some table scraps. He lifted me over the fence with the bowl of scraps. I stood there, and the two cows came running. They were bulls with horns. I became very frightened and thought that they would run over me. So I panicked and tried to climb the fence on my own. Then Grandpa's strong arms lifted me back over the fence to safety. He laughed a little and let me know there was nothing to be afraid of. He explained that the bulls were running up for the food, not to attack me. He then fed the bulls himself while I calmed down. I was old enough to be embarrassed, though, and this memory has stayed with me all these years.

It was good to remember my childhood days and the experiences at the farm. But most nights, alone in my apartment, I felt lonely. I felt like my problems were written all over my face. It was difficult to talk about my ex and say just enough so that people were satisfied. I couldn't tell them what he did, but I didn't feel right lying to them. I would only say that he had an affair. I felt like a failure, alone in my misery. I had to put on a good face for the people around me, but inside I was miserable.

I still thought about ending it all in suicide. The pain would be over; the lies would stop; and everyone could go about their business. Everyone seemed to have plenty of business; they were so busy with their own lives and problems that I couldn't talk to them about mine. The pain was great and the loneliness was worse.

I longed for someone to hold me and comfort me. I had tried to date some, back while my ex and I were separated and I lived in the old house, but I was rejected twice because of what my ex had done. Once the men found out what he did, they literally ran away from me. I did not want to go to bars to look for men, so I prayed to God over and over to ease my pain and loneliness. In bed at night, I would read until my eyes got sleepy. Many times before and after the divorce I would pray and ask God for guidance, then open the Bible and read whatever verse I came to and try to gain insight for myself.

One of the verses that kept popping up before the divorce was the one that states that I should not take a wife (*husband*), or have sons and daughters here. I took this to mean that I was not to stay in that city where I had lived with my ex and try to remarry or have any more children there. I was thirty-four years old and wanting a new life.

I also blamed myself for what had happened to Jozie. If only I had not given my ex that ultimatum to come back, he wouldn't have been around and nothing would have happened to my daughter. Guilt overwhelmed me, even though I knew that my ex did not have to choose to do what he did. But why couldn't I have prevented it? Why couldn't I have seen the signs before it happened? The only answer that I have ever been able to come up with is that I had no experience with this type of person or abuse. While teaching music in public school settings, I had not had to deal directly with the children's problems. I had grown up with an alcoholic father and was secluded from other children and what was going on in the world. I was in survival mode most of my life and not in tune with much else.

My ex was the first man that showed interest in me, and I thought that I was in love. We had met at a college party during my junior year. He had invited me to sit on his lap, and the rest is history. When he proposed to me, we were outside and chose a star that was ours.

At our wedding, I was nervous and had terrible sinus problems from allergies. I was standing with my dad in the parlor, ready to walk down the aisle, when out of nowhere, a loud male voice said, "No!" I asked my dad if he had said anything. He shook his head. I paused for a moment, looking around, and then dismissed the notion that I had heard anything at all. Now, looking back at this event, I am positive that God spoke to me that day.

During the days before the wedding, I had been filled with doubt. My parents didn't approve of my fiance or his family. I recall being confused and questioning my own motives. I would sit in the rocking chair in our living room and rock and rock and rock, not sure what to do. But I was also stubborn. I wanted to be married. I wanted to get away from my alcoholic father. I wanted to have fun.

I still went through with the wedding, because all those people where there, and I did not want to leave my groom at the altar. After the wedding, I forgot all about that voice until I moved into my new apartment, divorced, miserably alone, and suicidal. So I had yet another reason to blame myself for Jozie's abuse. If I had listened to that voice on my wedding day, I would not have married him, and Jozie would not have been molested. Of course, she wouldn't have been born either. I do thank God for my children and pray for them daily.

There had been a few times when I thought about divorcing my husband. One was early in the marriage, before we had children. We had had an argument about something, and my feelings had been hurt pretty badly. The thought of divorce crossed my mind, but it must have been a fleeting thought. After another argument, a few years later, I left the house and took a walk in the rain. But again, I did not leave him. The third time happened when he came back after his affair. We had had another argument, who knows about what, and I had decided to take a drive to be alone and try to clear my head. I drove to a nearby creek, parked the car, walked to the water's edge, and sat on a rock. It was almost dusk. I prayed and prayed. I kept asking God why He wanted me to get a divorce. I told Him over and over that I did not want to get a divorce. If I was to divorce my husband, I wanted to know why. I argued with God for more than thirty minutes. His response was always the same: "Get a divorce." My response was always "Tell me why." There was no answer. I finally gave up and decided to go home, because the mosquitoes were beginning to bite. I walked in the front door of the house, hung up my car keys on the wooden holder, and sighed a big sigh. No one was in the room, so I prayed calmly one last time. "Okay, God, why should I divorce my husband?" I asked. His answer came clear as day. "Because he is keeping you from doing My work." I blinked a couple of times and paused long enough for this to sink in. I have never forgotten that moment or the impact it had on me. God was always there. All I had to do was really listen to His will, not my own.

October 1991: Insults

The investigation of Jozie's molestation was not yet finished when we had moved away. Through my attorney, I received notice from the courts that I was not cooperating with the counseling bureau. And my ex wanted visitation rights. The counseling bureau wanted me to set up an appointment with them to discuss the case. They also wanted to know my current address, phone number, and place of employment. I guessed that I wasn't allowed to just disappear. The letter was mailed in mid-October, and it stated that I had until the end of November to respond with some form of communication.

I was frightened for my safety and that of my children's once more. If I let the bureau know where I lived, would they tell my ex? I put off calling them for a week. Then I decided that I had better do it. The minute that I got a hold of my case worker, she was pressuring me for my phone number, address, and place of employment. I was told that if I didn't give this information, the case would be closed and child support could stop. I didn't give her this information until the second phone call I made.

A few days later, my ex called me. Darn that bureau! They had told him where I was. He was pressuring me to cooperate with the counseling bureau. He made it sound like I was the bad guy the entire phone call. I'm not sure how he did this, but during the phone call he told me that he was on his way to my apartment. He must have been at a nearby pay phone. I told him not to come over, but he insisted on a visit.

When I hung up, I was in panic mode. I checked to make sure the chain and deadbolt were in place on the outside door. I had the kids go to the back bedroom, told them to stay there, and shut their door. I looked out the window and saw that it was dark and pouring rain. I was on the second floor, and the stairs were under a small alcove along with three other apartments' stairs and doors. Then came the knock at the door and my ex calling to me to let him in. He said again that child support might end if I didn't cooperate with the bureau. Through the closed door, I told him to go away. I told him that I understood his concern, but that I wanted him to leave. He asked to see the children. I told him they were fine. There was more said, but I don't recall what it was about. I do recall telling him to leave many times.

After a while, the man from the apartment across from mine came out of his door, and I heard him say to my ex, "I think that she wants you to leave." He may also have threatened to call the cops if my ex didn't leave. There was some conversation between them I could not understand, but eventually, my ex told me good-bye and left. From my window, I watched him go. Then I let my kids out of the back bedroom. I went out and knocked on my neighbor's door and thanked him for helping me out. That's another blessing from God above: the blessing of nice neighbors. After talking with my neighbor, I hugged my kids, and put them to bed. Sleep did not come easily for me that night.

Since the accusations of molestation were made, my ex and his family were always pressuring me to let them visit with the children. Back before the divorce was final and before I was able to move, they would call me and tell me how much they missed the children and ask if they were okay. I would call my friends and my marriage counselor and talk about what was going on with my case and what I was doing to protect my kids and myself. I knew I needed to talk to sane people. I needed to talk to people who really cared about me. I needed to talk to friends who could help me decide what to do. On more than one occasion, I called my friends, and the very next day, my ex called and asked me what I was up to. This would really freak me out. How did he know that I was planning something? Why did he ask me what I was up to? It seemed like he had bugged my phone and knew everything I had said.

Before the divorce, I had talked to the kindergarten teacher on my home phone. I thanked her for the letter she had sent to me about how Jozie had reacted to the video, and I asked if she would talk to me in person. I wasn't sure what to do and was asking her all sorts of questions. It was decided that I should talk to my attorney about my next move. The day after that phone call, my ex called me and the first words out of his mouth were "What are you up to?" I'm sure that I just talked about daily chores and whatnot, but this really scared me. This was another reason I got rid of my mother-in-law's car. It may have been bugged also. It was quite a relief for me when these types of phone calls stopped after I had moved away and changed my phone number.

Another insult for me was when I received a letter from my ex's new wife early in November after the divorce. She wanted to inform me of their recent marriage and that she was pregnant with his child, due in March 1992. Jozie had been born in March 1985. I prayed that this child would not be born on the same day as Jozie was. She also wrote of my ex's family missing my children and wanting to visit with them. More pressure.

Spring 1992:
Visitation Nightmares

Soon my ex started proceedings for his rights to visitation. In February 1992, I sent a letter to the counseling bureau with my spring break schedule in April to set up the visitation. I had acquired a long-term substitute position and did not want to miss any of it for this so-called visitation. In early March, I received two letters, one from the counseling bureau noting my schedule request and the other from my ex. His letter stated that he had already petitioned the court for either abatement or establishment of an escrow account for the child support. According to him and his attorney, I had not contacted the counseling bureau, even though I still have a letter from them stating that I had contacted them in February.

My ex was trying to stop paying child support. Plain and simple. He was forcing me to come back to his town and let him see his children. We were safe no more. He hadn't tried to contact us in person for a few months, but he had been busy with his attorney.

He had arranged a court date on March 13. I had to show up or lose two hundred dollars per week child support and a 2,500-dollar Christmas bonus. I was substituting, making only sixty dollars a day.

I contacted my attorney, who went to court for me and was able to get me more time. The ruling was that I had until April 3 to contact the bureau and agree to psychological testing. After that date, all child support would be escrowed, with another hearing scheduled for April 6. They wanted to evaluate me—a woman standing up for her daughter, a woman who made sure the abuse stopped once discovered, a woman who moved away and had to hide her family from the pressure of the abuser and his family. I was livid. It also appeared to me that the counseling bureau had not contacted the court about my communication with them back in February.

I was advised to contact yet another office to schedule this psychological testing. So I called and scheduled the testing for April 15 and 16, during my spring break. The evaluation would take approximately nine hours and the base cost would be 1,800 dollars. My ex would be responsible for all costs. An abuse expert was to be brought in to evaluate the people involved, and his cost alone would be eight hundred dollars. I don't know how my ex afforded all this, but he did.

I had to arrange for a hotel and drive the five hours one way to get there. I was not looking forward to it. I was nervous about the testing. Upon arrival, I had to leave my children in the next room with a counselor while I took the test. They were to be observed during a visit with their dad the next day. The test questions were simple and were sometimes asked again later in the test in a different way. The test took a couple of hours. I found out later that I passed with flying colors. I was normal. Great. Tell me something I don't know.

We got to leave and go back to the hotel. I had arranged for a visit with one of Jozie's best friends. We went out to supper and had a good time. The next day I was hesitant to let my children visit with their dad. A woman counselor introduced herself and said that she would be present the entire three hours. That, at least was somewhat comforting. I had to leave the building and was at a loss about what to do with myself. So, I went to a nearby park and walked around and swung on the swing set. While swinging, a memory of my youth came to me of swinging on our giant tree swing with our dad pushing us kids. We would try to tap the branches in front of us with our toes. Losing myself in the memory, I swung pretty high that day until a queasy feeling in my stomach reminded me where I was. I slowed down and got off the swing. Looking at my watch, I noticed that the three hours of visitation were almost up. When I went back to pick up my children, they seemed fine, and the visit went well. I was relieved, and the journey home was uneventful.

At about this time, I received a baby announcement from my ex. He had filled it out himself and signed it. They had their baby, a girl, on March 17. Not born on Jozie's birthday, yeah! He wrote a note in it stating that he wanted me to let our kids know that they had a sister. Wrong—the correct way to say that was stepsister. Why did he keep trying to keep communication alive between us? I never called or wrote to him at all. Maybe it was his way of wanting to brush what he did under the carpet and act like everything was normal. Whatever. I knew what he had done even if he continued to deny it.

They were escrowing my child support payments, so I was receiving no money from my ex. He was paying it to the court. Somehow the counseling bureau had not let the court know that I was cooperating with them. I had called them and told them where I was. I had contacted the psychological testing agency and set up the first appointment. I had left my children alone with my ex and a counselor for the first time since the divorce. The counseling bureau did not send any letter of information on my case to the court until May 12, 1992. This letter also stated that I had not responded to the court's order. But it did state that I had called that psychological testing agency to set up the appointment back in April.

June went by with no letters from any agency or my attorney or my ex. In July, the court, not the counseling bureau, ordered a review of child support set for August 12 at 1:30 p.m. My attorney also sent me a letter dated July 23 stating he was withdrawing from my case. I would have to go back to that town again, alone, and try to get my child support reinstated.

I was able to leave my son with a friend, but Jozie had to go with me on that five-hour drive. She was exhausted. I drove there and, at a local grocery-store copy machine, I copied all the papers from my files that I thought would help. I was confused and upset that I apparently had to defend my actions. By the time I had copied all the papers, I had a huge file.

I walked into the courtroom, dressed nicely, and loudly plopped down the file on my table. The judge, my ex, and the bailiff all looked at me. I tried to smile and look much more confident than I was. I was asked several questions, but the one that sticks in my mind was, "Why didn't you communicate with the counseling bureau?" I said that I had called them back in February. The court wanted to know why I was so hesitant to cooperate with any of the agencies associated with the case. I tried to show them the papers that I had run off. All the debt my ex had built up, all the times he was behind in child support, and all the letters showing that I had been cooperating.

But this did not seem to matter. The atmosphere in the courtroom was intense for me. I was at a loss. Then, almost in tears, I stated that my ex had come to the house and hit me and tried to take Jozie away one night before the divorce. The judge asked me if I had filed a police report. I said yes, but I didn't have a copy of it with me. The court took a short recess and must have looked this up. The judge returned, looked at me with concern, and rendered his decision. Everything had suddenly changed; the judge believed me. My ex was ordered to pay child support to me. All the money that was escrowed was mine. I had to agree to more supervised visitation and possibly more evaluations. I did. The court hearing was over. Jozie had been sitting in the back of the courtroom, so I went to get her, took her hand, and we left.

I had no more communication with the court, the counseling bureau, or my ex until one day in February 1993. My ex called me and said that he was done. I asked him what he was done with. He said he was done with visitation. He couldn't afford it. We talked a bit more, but when I hung up the phone, I cried. My ordeal was over. My ex would not be taking me back to court or to any more psychological testing. My children were safe. I was safe.

March 1993-June 1995:
A New School and Born Again

We moved to a different apartment, a townhouse. It was bigger than the other apartment, and it felt like a little house to me. The landlord let me install a security system on the front door, with the agreement that I would leave it there if I moved out. The new townhouse had a back door also, and the bedrooms were upstairs. It had a large eat-in kitchen, a bath and a half, and laundry facility. I had to purchase the washer and dryer, but I was happy to be doing laundry in my own apartment. We had two cats that my kids loved: Fluffy, a big, long-haired, mostly white cat, and Tiger, a mostly gray, short-haired, stripped cat. Jozie made new friends with some cute neighbor girls, and they usually included Danny when they played together. With the security system in place and my ex not informed of my move, I relaxed a bit and slept better.

I had been substitute teaching and landed a job in a local school system. The pay was good, and I now had benefits. Life was good. I even made friends with the parent of one of Jozie's new friends. We went to the local circus together and had a good time. We attended church and went to social gatherings. I still shared with people only that my ex had had an affair.

Jozie and I had some counseling after the move to the new state, but after a while, we needed to move on and start living. We celebrated holidays, went swimming in the neighborhood pool, played in the snow, and just enjoyed life. The only thing missing in my life was a man. Even with life being good, I was still lonely. I went to all of the church functions, and men were there, but none of them seemed interested in me. There was always someone prettier and thinner around for them to be seen with or the men were not attractive to me. I was a single parent who wanted to be married. I didn't know it then, but I would end up being a single parent for many years to come.

At the church I was attending, there was a local man who had a pro-life ministry. One Sunday he gave a talk and had a table out in the lobby with information about what he was doing and where local pro-life women's centers were located. That Sunday they also advertised in the bulletin a play about a woman who had had an abortion years earlier and was feeling guilty about it, knowing it was wrong. A friend recommended it, so I went.

I cried through the entire play because it brought back memories of my abortion in 1988. I was sixteen weeks along when, after a second ultrasound, the baby showed no signs of growing a cranium. The top of the baby's head was missing. I went to the hospital, and labor was induced with suppositories. I had not been feeling well during the pregnancy. The baby was actually dead inside me, and I was her life-support machine. Yes, the baby was a little girl. When she came out, the nurses took her away to clean her up. When they brought her back, I looked at her, and they asked me if I wanted to hold her. I shook my head and softly said no, so they took her away. But with that one look, I saw that she looked exactly like her father, my ex.

It was another blessing from God. God knew that I would have taken care of that baby if any other part of her body was deformed or missing. He knew that I would someday get divorced from my ex, and He gave me the blessing of not having to raise a child who looked like him. Instead, he blessed me, before I was ever aware, with my next child, my son, who looked more like me than my ex. Praise God!

Through this experience, seeing the play, and now the pro-life ministry at my church, I recommitted my life to God. I walked up to the display table in the lobby that Sunday and talked to the people behind it. I picked up pamphlets and information on Pro-Life Women's Centers in the area. I called a nearby center and started volunteering there one evening a week. They had babysitting available in their refinished basement, so I took my children with me.

Before all this, I had been pro-choice. Through praying and these activities, I became a pro-life advocate. I served for almost a year in a Women's

Center, and then God prompted me to stop serving in this capacity. During this time, I was also reading my new study Bible more and trying to memorize the order of the books of the New Testament. It took me a while, but I did it. I was singing in the church choir and participating in Christmas plays and Passion plays. These plays were fun, and I learned quite a bit about the life of Jesus. Both of my children were involved in Sunday school and the activities associated with it. Life was good.

I had paid off my Chapter 13 on my car by the end of 1993. Things were good, but I wanted a real house with a real yard for my children to play in. So I contacted a realtor, and we started looking at houses. We found one in the town where I had grown up. It was adorable. I signed the papers on New Year's Eve day of 1994, and we moved in. The neighbors were nice, and it was good to be in our own home. The house was a lot more work than the townhouse had been, but I kept my chin up and tried my best to keep everything in order.

Danny was in kindergarten, and Jozie was in fourth grade. They both had to change schools midyear. Danny seemed to handle the change well. Although Jozie liked her teacher, it was a difficult change for her. Jozie's teacher contacted me to come in for a conference. I walked into the classroom and was greeted by four teachers, Jozie's teacher among them. The room was decorated beautifully, with a huge forest display on one wall. One teacher closed the classroom door, I sat down in a chair, and we started the conference.

After just a few comments on how Jozie was doing, one of the teachers asked if Jozie had been molested. I was shocked. How did they know? How could they tell? Tears immediately welled up in my eyes. One of the teachers handed me a tissue. She said that Jozie displayed some of the behavior of a molested child. I admitted that this was true, but that it had stopped and I was divorced from her dad, the molester. I told them that there was a restraining order on him and that there was no contact between her dad and me. The conversation turned to other topics then, and I was thankful. It ended, and I went to the office and requested that I be the only person to pick up my kids from school. I went home and cried a bit in the privacy of my bedroom. It had been just another day in the life of a mom whose child was molested.

I decided to attend a local church that was just around the corner from our house. Through the church that we were attending, I learned of the benefits of being water baptized as an adult when you rededicate your life to Christ. I felt like I was born again already, but water baptism intrigued me, and I wanted to be a part of it. So, in June 1995, I took the born-again classes and was baptized in a tub of water in front of the congregation. The water was cold, and they dipped me three times during the ceremony. I was gasping for air by the third dip. It was quite a memorable event.

One of my friends at the church was extremely excited that day, because she had arranged for another one of my old friends to be there. This friend was the one who had led me to accept Jesus into my life back in English class my freshman year of high school. Yes, we sat and talked during English class, and I got saved. After the baptizing ceremony, both my friends were excited and happy for me, and it was nice to see my old friend again. I usually walked to church, so once I had changed into dry clothes, my old friend drove me and my children home. After that experience, I volunteered to help teach a Sunday school class. I was already serving in the choir. Life was good, but my aloneness was never more apparent.

My Insufferable Habit

When bad things happen to people, there can be a number of responses. Some people smoke, some eat too much, others do drugs, and some drink to ease their pain. Well, my response to the tragedy of losing my husband to another woman was to pull out my hair. I would sit alone and pull hairs out one by one. The more I pulled, the more it itched. The more it itched, the more I pulled. It was a vicious cycle. When he came back for a few months and left again, I pulled out my hair. When I received the letter from the kindergarten teacher telling me what Jozie had said to her after the video, I pulled out my hair. That was the worst time. I actually pulled so much that I could barely cover the baldness by parting it to one side. I knew when I was doing it, but I couldn't seem to stop.

Growing up, I had beautiful, long, brown hair. When I was in the fifth grade, it grew long enough for me to be able to sit on it. I had bangs, and whenever my hair was cut it always grew back. Then puberty came and worry, and when I was thirteen

I started this habit. Back then, it was minor, and my parents tried to help me stop. I kind of did. My graduation picture shows quite a lot of hair, but it is parted to one side. You see, I pulled my hair right from the top and left of my scalp. The pulling seemed to be associated with worry. Whenever I would worry about things, I would reach up and pull. My original wedding pictures also show my hair parted to one side, and the veil helped cover the baldness. Through the years, my hair would grow back when I was pregnant. Then I would do some damage by pulling some out again.

After I was born again and baptized, I prayed and prayed, asking God to take this habit away. He did, but I guess the damage had become permanent. There was no hair growing back anymore, and I was only in my mid-thirties. I visited a dermatologist, and he said my scalp was healthy. He suggested using an over-the-counter hair re-growth ointment. I tried it, and one small section did grow back. I used the ointment off and on, when I could afford it, but after that first growth spurt, nothing seemed to be happening. I was extremely self-conscious of my baldness and wore a barrette to hold my hair in place to cover the baldness.

Whenever I went to amusement parks with my children, I wore cute ball caps to cover it so I could ride the water rides. On windy days, I would also wear caps or use a lot of hairspray and a barrette to hold my hair in place. When I got parts in play at a local theater, I usually played a much older part because my hair was thin and parted on the side.

And the sad truth is that men would look at me and think that something was wrong with me because of my hair's thinness. True, my weight would fluctuate throughout the years, but men would look at me, look at my hair, and then look away. So not only had my daughter been molested by my husband, but with my hair looking the way it did, I didn't stand a chance with men. It took me a long time to realize this. Looking back at family pictures, I can see it clearly. But while I was living it, I always held on to the hope that I would not always be alone or partly bald.

1995 to 1997:
My Lunch Truck Experience

God told me to leave the school system that I was teaching in. Just up and leave it. So, at the end of the school year, in June 1995, I quit my job. I started waitressing for a local catering business. It also had a lunch truck that an employee would drive around to local businesses to sell coffee, sandwiches, snacks, juice, pop, and so forth to employees on their lunch break. The driver of the lunch truck was leaving, so I asked if I could try it. I went through a training session, and I passed. My pay was increased, so I was a happy camper.

During the first year that I drove the truck, I increased sales by more than a half. I would notice where businesses were that we had not been stopping at and go work them into my schedule. This made my boss happy with me. It seemed a good fit for me also because I was in my own hometown, I was also close to my children, and I could wear a cap with the job and look pretty normal. Most of the stops were men customers, and I did have a few offers, but

I only went out with one man from one company. It didn't work out because he was quite a bit older than me. Most of the men were married with children anyway.

One of my stops was at a local mechanic shop. The man who owned this shop became my mechanic too. He was a good man who worked hard and knew cars. To me he was like a second dad. He would fix any problem that my car had and tease me every time I stopped at his shop. He was also married.

At this same time, spring of 1997, I auditioned for a part in a musical at the local theater and got it. I had a blast. I played the part of a sister to the leading actress. I sang and spoke my lines with energy. We performed fifteen shows that summer with standing ovations at several of them.

Then one hot day in the summer of 1997, I was driving the lunch truck on my usual route; I had been driving the lunch truck job for about two years. I was tired from all the heat and early mornings. At one stop, I left the side door open. And I forgot to close it when I drove away from the stop. All was well until I had to park for the next stop. I pulled alongside the sidewalk, and there was a telephone pole right in my line of parking. I stopped and then noticed that I wasn't even with the front door of the store I was to enter. So I pulled forward a little bit, and the open side of the truck hit the telephone pole. The door crinkled. I backed up the truck, parked it, and got out. I looked at the pole. No damage. Then I looked at the truck door and couldn't believe my eyes.

It was crinkled so badly that I could not shut it all the way. I lost my temper and was kicking the tire of the truck when a customer came out to see what was going on. I thought it a good time to control myself. She talked to me a bit, then I went to my next stop. One of the guys there tried to shut the door. He had a little more success than I did.

Then the full realization of what I had done hit me, and I started to cry. I would lose my job. I was done. The door would need to be replaced, and I would have to pay for it. I slowly drove the truck back to the catering shop and let the owner know what had happened. He was upset at first, but I didn't lose my job and I didn't have to pay for the door.

This also brings to mind the time I slid off a narrow, slippery road during the winter before, and the truck and I ended up in a field. I was driving slowly, but a van came along, and I got too far over to let it pass me. I tried to stay on the road, but the shoulder was too slippery, and the truck slid off of it. I avoided hitting a speed-limit sign and came to a full stop about fifty feet into the field. The truck was fine, but it had to be pulled out of the field with a tow truck. I praised God for an understanding boss.

I also took a job delivering newspapers from four to six in the morning. I thought it would be great, running from door to door, getting exercise, and being paid at the same time. But this newspaper job actually wore me out and put stress on my eyes, because it was dark out there delivering newspapers. I used a flashlight, but my eyesight started to go, and I had to get reading glasses.

With this extra income, I also managed to pay for a trip to a Florida fun park for my family. We had fun, but it was a little chilly as I recall. Near the end of my time driving the lunch truck and delivering newspapers, I was so tired and in a hurry to finish my paper route that I left my van in gear in someone's driveway when I jumped out of it to put the newspaper in their door. The van crept up to their garage door and dented it in while I delivered the newspaper. I left my phone number in their mailbox and ended up paying for a new garage door for them. I was seriously considering quiting delivering newspapers.

1997: Forty Years Old and Back to Teaching

I t was the summer of 1997, and I was at a Christian bookstore with my children. I was in one aisle with Danny, looking at some books, and Jozie was in another aisle. One of Jozie's substitutes from her school happened to be there, and she spoke with Jozie. After she left, I asked Jozie what they talked about. She had asked Jozie how she was and how her summer was going. She also mentioned to Jozie that there was a job opening in another town—a music position at the elementary school.

I took this as a sign from God that I was supposed to apply there. I was so excited! I went home, worked on my resume, put together a file, and applied. I was a little late for my interview, because my catering boss would not let me off early to get there. I had to shower and change and drive more than twenty minutes to get there. I apologized to the principal, and she said she didn't mind.

The interview went well, but I did not get the job. They decided to hire a young man right out of college who was known in the community. A month later, I saw another ad in the local newspaper asking for substitutes, so I applied and was called almost every day in my hometown. That's when I was able to quit my lunch truck job. I worked as a substitute until January 1998.

Then I got a phone call from the other town where they had hired that young man right out of college. He had quit on them in December. They needed someone immediately. Thank you, Lord! I interviewed and got the job. It was part time, but I was okay with that. This job paid more than the newspaper delivery and the lunch truck jobs combined. I was able to deliver newspapers early in the morning and then report to the school around ten.

With all of these financial changes, I felt that it was time to purchase a newer car. I looked at a used-car dealership, I test drove a Jeep that was red and wonderful. I was sitting up high, and I felt like I ruled the road. The Jeep was a 1996 and fun to drive. I traded in my old van, and we were good to go. Or so I thought.

Near the end of January, child support stopped arriving. It just stopped without warning. No letter or phone call. I called my ex's employer to speak to him, and they told me he didn't work there anymore. They had to tell me twice, because I couldn't believe it. I didn't have a phone number for him, so I called his mother. She told me that she didn't know where he was. I felt ill. I called the child support agency, and they told me he had lost his job.

So I was on my own. I found out much later that my ex had been in a domestic dispute with his wife at the time. She had taken an ax to him and cut his leg. He had ended up in jail for a while. He claimed that she had been drunk during the dispute. After all the trouble, he moved back in with his parents, his wife disappeared, and their daughter was put in a foster home. I found out that my ex's sister had to take over the sale of the house he had been living in, and she had quite a mess to clean up after their dispute.

Wow. I'm wondering now if his wife had noticed what I had noticed when I was married to him and if their child had been put through the same abuse that my daughter had. Their daughter would have been five years old at the time. The similarity of the both girls' ages and problems with both of our marriages seemed uncanny. If I could have taken an ax to him and gotten away with it, I would have. I know right where I would have aimed. Shame on me. Oh well.

So I quit my newspaper delivery job and got a job at a fast-food shop in town. I needed more pay and longer hours. True, I missed my kids, but the Jeep cost money, and I didn't want to go through another Chapter 13. I had to work and pay for everything. It was now my job alone.

I continued to call and write to the child support agency back in the state where the divorce was finalized. They were either on the other line, away from their desk, or supposedly working on my case. I tried to work with them for over six months, but nothing came of it. A friend suggested that I try contacting the local child support agency and let them work with the out-of-state agency. I gave this tactic a try, and it worked. It took until the month of October, but I finally received a check for about forty-eight dollars. I couldn't believe it. I was so surprised that I called the local agency and thanked them for helping me. True, the check was tiny, but from my perspective I had won a battle. My ex was paying child support again, even if it was much reduced. The payments increased to ninety-two dollars and some change every two weeks. Through the years, these payments have stayed the same. True, they weren't much, but every bit helped a single mom to make ends meet.

My teaching job was going great, and in the fall of 1998 I went to full-time employment. Both of my children seemed to be doing fine. They both played soccer and baseball. Their grades in school were good. Jozie had been in a couple of local beauty pageants. We were active in our churches activities. I was being chosen to sing a solo here and there at church. I was able to participate in several Christmas extravaganzas and Easter Passion plays. We celebrated birthdays with sleepovers for Jozie and backyard parties for Danny.

In all, we had a decent life. I was able to cover my baldness with my hair parted on the side and with the use of my handy, ever-present barrette. We had fun at the nearest water park and amusement park. I was the designated camera person for all the fun. I didn't mind.

Well, the title of this chapter is "Forty Years Old and Back to Teaching." So I guess that I should address the issue of turning forty before going on to the next chapter. I was married when I was twenty-two, divorced when I was thirty-four, and still single six years later at age forty. My family had thrown a nice surprise party for me. I was a devoted mother, but I dreamed of being married. I had heard from somewhere that for every year that you were married it takes the same amount of years again to get over it and to be ready to move on to another relationship. I had been married eleven years (I don't count the year it took to finalize the divorce). If this was true, I had about five years to go, and I would be forty-five. It seemed like eternity.

I felt like I had quite a bit to offer a man. I could cook, clean, install new hallway lights, install a dimmer switch, paint the entire outside of a house, lay kitchen tile, weed, and take care of perennials, work two jobs at a time, make it to all of my children's soccer games and band concerts, teach private music lessons, redecorate and remodel a bathroom (with my brother's help), turn a one-car garage into a bedroom (with a lot of help from a friend's husband, a contractor), and still have time to walk the dog.

I was a busy lady, but I had time to go to the occasional Friday-night singles dance at church. I had always wanted the family life. I wanted my children to have a dad—a good dad, a man to show them who and how to be. I tried to remain hopeful, but my children and I were only getting older. I had read all sorts of books on the topics of dating and the differences between men and women. I even made a list of what I thought my 'man' should be like. But, nothing seemed to help. I did have a few dates and one longer relationship, but nothing that was lasting.

One gentleman I knew (our boys were friends) pegged the reason for my being alone and truly why I had not met the right person yet. I wanted to go out with him, but he said he was much more of a partier than I was. He really didn't know me. He had only met me a couple of times. I think he could tell that I needed a God-fearing man. I did need a man who believed in God, but I'm not sure how he could tell this. Maybe it was from my demeanor, my actions, or my words. I don't know.

Looking back now, I can see that God had me in the palm of His hand and that I was in waiting. It was a difficult, lonely, and painful waiting. I had to make all the decisions about everything and be everything to both of my children. I feel like I tried so hard to be and do all of this.

1998-2001:
Life Choices and Changes

My children were growing up. Jozie was now twelve and Danny was eight. Jozie loved horses, so for her birthday I scraped five hundred dollars together and bought her a quarter horse. She joined a 4-H club and took care of and showed her horse for the next couple of years. Danny was still in elementary school and decided to participate in the school talent show. He had just started playing his recorder in music class, so he chose to play it for the talent show. The show was near St. Patrick's Day, so I dressed him up in a white shirt, blue jeans, a green vest, and a black top hat with a green clover on it. He didn't win anything, but he played his recorder well and had a good time.

In the fall of 1998, we were attending a church that was offering a baptism class and ceremony. With my children watching, I had been baptized, so I suggested to them that they should be baptized too. The class included children, so we attended it. It came time for the ceremony, and we were all looking forward to it. Both of my children were to wear white robes and be baptized in the large pond in the backyard of the church. It was near the end of September, and the pictures I took show that the trees were just starting to turn. The water was waist deep and chilly.

The pastors took good care of my children, and the ceremony was completed. I asked both children if they had felt anything while they were being baptized. Jozie didn't say much, but Danny said that he felt Jesus rushing into his heart. *Wow*, I thought. I smiled and hugged both of them. This treasured memory has stayed with me all these years, and I hope that I never forget it.

Time flew by, my job was going well, and my children seemed fine. In the spring of 1999, I decided to audition for another musical at the local theater. I danced and sang for them, and I got a principle part. I was *so* excited. We practiced and practiced and performed fifteen shows near the end of July.

One of my sisters came to one of the performances. The theater was quite small. While I was performing one of my scenes, out of the corner of my eye, I caught her leaning over and laughing. This encouraged me, and I really gave the scene my all. When I finished the scene and went backstage, one of the other performers commented to me that my acting was "over the top" that time. Thank you, sister! The cast was great, and we had fun, family-oriented cast parties. I have always loved performing in local musicals. I get to act and sing and still be a mom.

I kept wondering how and if I should tell my children what their dad had done. All I ever said to them was that he hurt us and that we don't have contact with him at all. But now my children were older. Jozie was turning into a beautiful young lady. Danny was a fun-loving young man. I wanted to tell them, but never knew how. One day, in the summer of 2000, I asked them if they might want to visit with their dad.

Through his sister, I knew that my ex had also moved to his hometown, and I was able to reach him. Before the issue of the visitation ending in 1993, he had notified me of his move back home also. We both now lived in the same state, our home state, where we had grown up, gone to college, and met. Back before the visitation was settled, I had arranged visits with him in public restaurants. I thought that I had to do this to please the court and keep the child support coming. I never shared with him where I lived, and I always drove a couple of towns away to meet him. He only had my phone number. We had these visits, usually around someone's birthday or near Christmas.

Back in that time, I was in counseling also. One counselor suggested that I confront my ex and tell him how much he had hurt me. So I did. I had arranged to meet my ex at a restaurant around Christmas. He brought his sister with him, and the meal went fine with mostly eating and small talk. There was no opportunity to confront him. At the end of the meal, my ex stated that he had some gifts for the kids in the trunk of his car. He went out to his car, and I saw my opportunity. I left the kids with his sister and followed him to his car. While we were gathering up the gifts from his trunk, I took a deep breath and told him that what he did had really hurt me, just the way I had practiced with my counselor. He did not apologize. He only said that I was a good person and that I deserved to be happy. That was basically it for that confrontation, and we went back into the restaurant with the gifts.

Another time, I believe it was Christmas, 1995, I had to drive to his house, where he lived with his parents, to collect my portion of his bonus check. He was not inclined to mail it to the court so they could mail it to me. I wanted it before Christmas so I could buy gifts for my kids. I was very nervous. I was hoping for a smooth visit, but it seemed to me that I was walking into the lions' den or that the visit would compare to the story of David and Goliath; my ex's family were my Goliath.

I decided to keep the visit short and tag a visit to a nearby zoo onto the time allowed for the trip. This would give me an excuse to stay for a short period and leave as soon as I saw an opening. When I walked into the house, the mood was tense and the conversation was strained, but there were no confrontations of any kind. This was probably due to the children being present. After what seemed to me like an eternity, my ex handed me the check. I thanked him and as soon as I could, gathered up my children, and left. We went to the zoo and had a good time.

Those visits were stressful for me, but I put up with them. Early on, when the visits were arranged, my ex would call me, wanting to see the kids. I recall asking friends, male and female, to go with me so that I would not have to face my ex alone. I would explain the situation and the abuse, and the supposed friend would usually take a deep breath, look away from me, and say that they couldn't go. I recall asking several times and several different friends to help, only to be turned down each time. After a while, I learned to stop asking and just go to those visits by myself.

So, getting back to the year 2000, I had asked my children if they wanted to see their dad, and they said yes. This time, though, I was calling the shots; I was not driving for over an hour one way just so my ex could see his children. And there had been no recent pressure from him or his family to take the children for any reason. So I invited him to come to my house for a Halloween pumpkin-cutting experience with his children. He came, I took pictures, and a good time was had by all.

The children seemed to enjoy being with their dad. Jozie was pretty quiet during the visit, but Danny talked, smiled, and joked with his dad. I was glad to see this, but I was still cautious about what I said and did. I'm really not sure why I arranged that party. Maybe I kept hoping for him to admit the abuse and apologize. I guess I needed this for closure, but an apology didn't come and still hasn't come.

Meanwhile, more fun family things were going on. Jozie was taking private voice lessons and sang beautifully in her recitals. Danny was involved in soccer full tilt. My job was going well. I was also teaching private voice and piano lessons and holding recitals for my students. We always had cats in the house as pets, along with our family dog.

Jozie was now in high school and joined the band color guard. The school band was an award-winning one, and they went to several band competitions during the band season and received first-place ratings. In 2001, the band also went to the district competition and received the top rating. I served in the concession stand with all the other band parents. I also went to see all of Danny's home soccer games. Jozie also started playing tennis her sophomore year, and when she was a junior, she was just good enough to play on the varsity level. Life was full and busy.

In the summer of 2001, I noticed an ad in the local newspaper for a music director at a local church. I decided to apply and got the job. So now I had a full-time teaching job at an elementary school during the week, about twenty students in my private studio, and a weekend job leading music at the local church. Busy was now my middle name. I was so happy to be involved in music almost every waking hour. My children seemed happy and busy also.

My son helped me set up and tear down the hand-bell tables before and after practice. He also attended church and Sunday school class. Jozie, however, did not participate at church much at all. She had many band practices and some performances on Sundays. She had tennis matches early on many Saturdays and only came to church on Sundays here and there.

During that summer, Jozie met a boy at the local bowling alley. She was smitten with him. I thought that I was keeping her busy with all her activities, but I was wrong. One day, late in October, Jozie was in her bedroom when I came home from work. She was upset about something. I opened her bedroom door and asked her what was wrong. She told me she was pregnant.

I was shocked and overwhelmed. She was a junior in high school. Sixteen years old. I asked her if she was sure. She said she was. But I was unable to comfort her. I went to my room, closed my bedroom door, lay on my bed, and cried.

2001-2004:
Grandma Too Young

I sat at Jozie's last band performance of the season and cried. The tears flowed. I could not seem to stop them. She looked so beautiful in her outfit. Even though she was a few months pregnant, she was not showing yet. She finished her tennis season also. She had been playing her best tennis ever.

My lovely, dark-haired, hazel-eyed firstborn was pregnant. I was so angry and disappointed. I had such high hopes for her: college, career, then marriage and kids. She had expressed the desire to become a veterinarian. I was so sad that I could not hide my tears. My heart was breaking again. She had needed a dad so badly—someone to protect her, love her, and let her know that she was important. I was not enough. I had turned forty-four that year. I was way too young to be a grandma.

Jozie would have to finish high school. There was no question about that. She would have to go to school while she was pregnant. We had discussed abortion, and Jozie had stated that she could not kill the life within her. Since I had become born-again, changed to a pro-life believer, and served in the women's center, I had to agree with her.

I made sure that she had medical care and clothes to fit her growing body. She took good care of herself. She watched pregnancy shows on television, and she even listened to classical music while drifting off to sleep at night. She participated in the science fair that year, and I recall that she placed well enough to go to the district competition. Her teachers were all nice to her and concerned for her welfare. She also sang in her school choir concert that year.

Jozie's pregnancy went well. She had a couple of false labor episodes, but otherwise no complications of any kind. She had a little boy early in June that year. She was allowed three people at her bedside during the birthing process. I was there, along with the baby's dad and Jozie's closest girlfriend. The child was beautiful, healthy, and born with a head full of black hair. I got the honor of changing his first diaper. Yes, it was black and smelled awful, but I didn't care. I was a grandma. Even though the circumstances weren't the best, I was happy.

The baby's dad was there and seemed happy also. I was stressed to see him because I had banned him from seeing Jozie while she was pregnant. They were both sixteen at the time she had gotten pregnant. I was her mom. I could order such things if I saw fit. The dad had actually obeyed me and stayed away from my daughter.

Now the real work began. My house only had two actual bedrooms. A utility room had been added onto the back of the garage before I had bought the house. I decorated this room for the baby. We painted it light blue, and the curtains and pictures on the wall were of bears in overalls. Jozie had a baby shower at her closest girlfriend's house, and she had received a bassinet at this shower. At first, the baby slept with Jozie in her bedroom in the bassinet. But as he grew, he slept in the utility room in his crib.

With the help of a friend from church, we turned the garage into a bedroom for Danny. There was no heat in it, so I bought portable space heaters that didn't blow heat but only heated up the area around them. We kept his door shut to keep the heat in. During the summer, I put in a window air-conditioner to keep the garage comfortable. With five people living in an originally two-bedroom home, my house was full. Every bit of space was used.

Jozie needed to finish her senior year at high school. So I helped her arrange baby-sitting. The baby-sitter was on my way to work, so I took on this responsibility of driving her son to the baby-sitter in the morning and picking him up on my way home.

Imagine my concern about paying for essentially three children now. Danny was only thirteen at the time and in middle school. Jozie was seventeen, and her son was almost three months old when she needed to go to school that fall. So I helped her to apply for any government assistance she could. These programs were helpful, but they did not pay the electric, water, or gas bills. All of my utilities increased, and I was also paying for the day care expenses. I also bought Jozie her first car back in March of 2001 when she had just turned sixteen. She was supposed to help pay for the car, but I ended up paying for it almost entirely. She did get a part-time job at a local fast-food restaurant, but it didn't pay much. Money was tight, and the debt I had was not going away. Minimum payments were all I could afford.

My mother was supportive to me, gave gifts for my grandson at the baby shower, and came to birthday parties I sponsored for him in the years to come. Family gatherings were difficult. My family wanted to be supportive, but mostly they ignored me and my growing family. My dad passed away in October of 2001, never having seen his great-grandchild. He probably would have been critical and judgmental of me and my daughter, because he always was that way.

So, with all this going on, guess what! I didn't have time for a man in my life at all. By the time I dropped off my grandson, went to work, picked him up, went home, took care of supper, taught private lessons, and worked at the church on weekends, I was exhausted. I was in my mid-forties, a single mom and a grandma with way too much baggage for any normal man to put up with. I had been dating someone in the months before Jozie got pregnant, but that relationship ended during the summer before her pregnancy.

Financially, I was managing, but the stress was great. I felt old and worn out and unworthy of a relationship. My parenting skills must have been very lacking, but I could not see it. Danny has said that his sister ruined his life with her pregnancy. His embarrassment must have been great, and he probably felt ignored during that time in his life. He had become an uncle at the ripe old age of thirteen, and his nephew lived with him.

I tried to keep on top of everything, and mostly I did. The dishes got done (we didn't have an automatic dishwasher), laundry was always going, and my job was going okay. Danny's school grades were still good, and so were Jozie's. I had installed new living-room carpet and a new kitchen floor.

I tried to show Jozie how to be a good mom and take care of her son. I'm not sure how she felt about having a son, though I could tell that she loved him. But it seemed no matter how hard I tried, she and I did not see eye to eye. To me she was rebellious; she thought she could move out whenever she wanted to and do whatever she wanted. We argued about this quite often, and I would always ask her how she was going to pay for it. My challenge to her was that if she moved out, she would have to pay for the car and insurance herself. We even had a meeting with my pastor to reason with her that she could not afford to live by herself.

There were a couple of occasions when she decided to run away with her son. One I remember in particular. I was teaching piano lessons one cold night during the winter after he had turned one year old. Jozie packed up the baby bag, put her son in his winter coat, and walked down to a nearby bus stop. Danny told me this after she had left. I couldn't go after her, because I was committed to the piano lesson I had right then; the student was a child, so I couldn't ask him to leave. So I finished the lesson and had another lesson already scheduled.

During that second lesson, Jozie came back to the house with her son. They came in the back door and then went into Danny's bedroom. Danny told me they were back. I immediately excused myself from the lesson and went to the bedroom. Jozie had forgotten to put gloves on her son's hands, and they were red and cold. I treated his hands, and Jozie said that he had cried the entire time they were waiting on the bus. I'm not sure what I said to Jozie at the time. I had to get back to my piano lesson. After the piano student left, Jozie and I exchanged angry words. I scolded her for taking my grandson out in the cold. She said that he was fine and closed her bedroom door on me.

So many times I wanted to order her out of my house. So many times I wanted to wash my hands of her and her bad manners. Her bedroom was always a mess, with clothes and junk strewn everywhere— so much so, that a person couldn't walk in her room without stepping on clothes or junk. But every time I thought this through, I knew I could not kick her out. I had a grandson, and his safety and well-being were too important to me.

I don't know when or how, but shortly after she graduated, Jozie met another man. When he came over to the house, she was excited and happy to see him. He seemed okay to me, although I did have some reservations about him. She moved in with him, and they lived in a house that they rented. The rent and the utilities were in Jozie's name. Not a good sign. I found out through my visits with my grandson that this man was cruel to him. He played mean tricks on him, and my grandson told me that he always felt safer when his mom was there at the house with him. I spoke to Jozie about this, to no avail.

I also learned that there were many drinking parties, and when I visited their house, many empty beer bottles would be in their trash and near the back door. The man was a drunk. Plain and simple. Meanness and cruelty were his middle name. Unfortunately, Jozie got pregnant again. Her excuse this time was that she ran out of birth control pills. She and her son moved back home. I was relieved for my grandson's safety, but angry at her for getting pregnant again. Didn't she learn anything from her first pregnancy? I did a lot of scolding, but still agreed to help her out again.

Again we discussed abortion. We both agreed that she and I could not afford another child. We went to an abortion clinic, but I refused to go in. She went in by herself and got information and an appointment. While she was in the clinic, I was praying and asking God if we should go through with it. I recall asking God that, if we were not to, he would show me a Christian women's shelter nearby. I opened my eyes from praying, looked across the alley, and saw it: a women's shelter. I knew what they were about, since I had served in one.

When Jozie came out of the abortion clinic, I showed her the women's shelter. She did not want to go in. I went in by myself. I got information on how a baby is formed in the womb. They also told me that they could do an ultrasound of the baby right there, if Jozie would come in. So I took the information out to Jozie and told her what they had said. She agreed to go in and have the ultrasound.

The ultrasound was performed, and we found out that the baby was a girl and healthy. I think Jozie was excited to be having a girl, but I was totally upset. We got back in the car, and I scolded Jozie up and down about responsibility and consequences of foolish decisions. She listened but was busy eating a chicken sandwich. I don't know if any of what I said sunk in.

She lived with me while she was pregnant and was also working at a fast-food establishment. I tried to help her take good care of herself during this pregnancy also. Now, looking back at this time, I wonder why she didn't stay with that man during her pregnancy. I'm still not sure why she had to live with me. She was an adult, over eighteen, supposedly able to make 'adult' decisions. Maybe that man didn't want her living with him while she was pregnant. Maybe she didn't tell him right away, afraid of his reaction. Whatever the case, she lived with me and worked. Jozie stayed pretty much to herself during those months of her pregnancy, and we argued very little.

While Jozie was pregnant, I had some fun of my own. I auditioned and got another principle part in another musical soon to show at the local theater. I had a blast; I had several lines and a solo, and I sang with a group of ladies. I would cook a large supper for my family and then off to rehearsal I would go. I was in quite a few scenes and really enjoyed it. We performed fifteen shows during that summer of 2004. But it was over too soon, and the summer went by all too quickly.

The day of Samantha's birth came in early December, and the delivery was normal. But right after she was born, Samantha was lethargic and was whisked off to intensive care and kept there for more than five hours. The nurses kept her on a heart monitor and called us on the phone in Jozie's room, telling us that everything was fine and that they had other emergencies to deal with. I was allowed to look in the window of the intensive care unit, but when I looked for Samantha, I could not see her.

They finally let Jozie and me go into the unit to see her. She looked all right, but we found out later that she might have suffered a stroke and had a hole in her left temporal lobe. Samantha had cerebral palsy and was legally blind; she couldn't talk or walk. She was wheelchair bound and grew, but she did not get better. Samantha has gone to be with her Maker now. Since Samantha is not the topic of this book, I will not elaborate any more on her or her passing.

Samantha's dad was present at her birth in 2004, but shortly after she was born, he had to go back to work, and we were left alone at the hospital. We did establish his parental status, and Jozie eventually moved back in with him. They would come and visit me, and the visits were okay, but stressful for me.

That man had a mean streak in him, and some of his comments were disrespectful to Jozie and me. I chose to avoid him and responded only to Jozie's phone calls to me.

So, as you can tell, I was a grandma way too young and totally in the wrong manner. Jozie had two children from two different dads. She was unmarried and in two different relationships that did not work. Growing up, she had no example of what a good relationship was, since I was by myself for so long. When she had her son, I had been alone for eleven years; when she had her daughter, I had been alone for thirteen years.

Believe me, I had tried to meet my special someone, but most of my relationships didn't last past two months. Before Jozie had her son, I dated someone who I thought I might marry, but he was eight years older than me and would not commit to a serious relationship. Something in his past was bothering him, and he would not tell me what it was. He chose to turn me away so many times that I finally gave up on him.

2004-2005:
Depression and Desperation

I was depressed. For how long, I don't really know for sure. I would fix my hair and feel shame. I would look at my lonely life and feel sad. I would look at my children and feel stress. I would pray to God continually about these things, and nothing seemed to be getting any better. I went on dating sites online. One website matched me to a pastor who never even winked at me. I went to Christian singles dances and had a great time, but never met the right man for me. I was reading Christian magazines and books on dating, and going out with my single-lady friends to movies. But I was always alone going home.

After I had been dating online for about two years, I was angry and let God know it. I told Him I was going to a bar. I practically yelled this at Him. I was fed up. So I went to a bar in the next town that I considered to be nice enough and safe enough for me. I sat there on a barstool for an hour and talked to no one. Finally a man came into the bar and sat next to me. We didn't speak for quite a while.

At the back of the bar, off to one side, they started singing karaoke. It was awful. To me, there is nothing worse than listening to bad karaoke. I decided to leave and wasn't sure how to leave a tip. So I asked the man next to me how much tip I should leave. Then we talked for about thirty minutes. I'm not sure what we discussed. Most of it was small talk about what we did for a living and such. The more we talked, the more I realized I was not supposed to be at that bar. I would look around occasionally and see more and more people coming into the bar. Most of them were young folks in their twenties and full of youth and energy.

The man that I was talking to was almost as old as me, but I didn't feel any chemistry with him, and the conversation dragged. I finally made up some excuse to go and left. I got back to my car and apologized to God. True, one of my Christian friends had met her future mate at a bar, but it wasn't the right setting for me. Both she and her mate had been invited by friends to the bar, and it was the first time either of them had gone there. They are still married and very happy. No such luck for me. I went back to my online dating sites and kept looking.

My depression seemed to overwhelm me. I was angry, alone, and approaching fifty years old. I would look back at my life and wonder where it went. It seemed that I gave the best years of my life to my ex and his happiness. Being a single parent, all I did was work and attend to the issues of daily life.

During that time, I read a Christian magazine that had stories about people that were depressed. As I read about them I began to realize that I was like them. Each time I read another story about their depression and how they overcame it, my desire to change grew. But I wasn't sure how to do it. How could I overcome my depression? I was a busy woman. I had my children; and people who told me this thought it comforted me. Oh, but I felt alone. God had blessed me with two children, but I was still alone. My son would soon be graduating from high school and going to college. My daughter was out living with a man again. Where did that leave me? Alone.

So, I began to do what the people in the magazine did. I prayed to God. I prayed every day and night that He would lift my depression. I prayed that since I finally recognized what was going on with me it should be no more. I prayed that my depression would cease and desist. I'm not sure anymore how many weeks or months I prayed for this.

One night I was kneeling at my bedside praying. My bedroom door was open, and no one else was home. I was facing my bed with my back to the door, praying my usual prayer filled with praises and then with my concerns. With my eyes closed, I felt a presence in the house. This presence was moving down the hallway toward me. I knew that the house was locked up, because I had locked it myself.

I stopped praying and turned and looked behind me, but saw nothing. No shadow, no noise. It felt to me as if the presence merely stopped and waited. A small voice in my head suggested that I was not to be afraid and that I should resume praying. Slowly I turned back to the business of praying. I closed my eyes tightly and tried to focus on my prayers. Then I felt the presence approach me and encircle me as I was praying. I kept my eyes closed, my head bent and my hands folded as long as I could.

After a short while, but what seemed like an eternity, I felt the presence leave, and I opened my eyes. I smiled for no reason at all. Then I began to laugh. I laughed a belly laugh like I had never done before. I giggled, I sighed, and then I laughed some more. I laughed so hard I cried. It was like I had a bad case of the giggles and couldn't stop. I had no reason to laugh, but I was laughing.

I got up from the floor, and my laughter continued. I sat on my bed and laughed some more. I probably laughed for a good twenty minutes. I walked around the house to check for any open doors or to see if anything was out of place, and nothing was. The giggling finally subsided, and I went to bed.

The next day I realized what had happened. The Holy Spirit had come to visit me and lifted my depression. From what I had read about the Holy Spirit, I was certain that I had experienced a divine intervention. My mood was better. Life didn't seem so horrible. I stopped complaining to God about every little thing. I began to notice the little daily blessings God provides. I tried to see things from other people's perspective.

I had always maintained hope that my life would get better and that I would not end up alone. Now I felt it in my heart that it was only a matter of time before I would meet my special someone. God had also broken down my narrow view of life where I only thought of myself and no one else. My blinders were destroyed, and I began to notice how a lot of people had it worse than I ever did. True, I was alone. But God had been trying to tell me all along that He is my father, that I am never alone, and that I am not in control, even when I think I am.

He is my joy, and I am to look to Him for everything. He loves me no matter what. The journey with God never ends, and He will never forsake me.

2005:
Higher Education and
a Short Vacation

With the shift in my attitude and with the needs of my family changing, I decided to get my master's of music education degree. A nearby college was offering summer classes for music teachers. I could feasibly take three summers of classes, complete a graduation project, and graduate in May of 2008. If I completed that degree, my pay would increase, and I could apply for tenure. So I took the plunge. I visited the college and got all the information to register. Along with a song in English, I would have to prepare songs in three other languages and sing an audition to be accepted into the master's program.

I also would need an accompanist. I was still working at the church as the choir director, so I asked one of the church's accompanists to play for me. He agreed to play for me for a reasonable fee. We worked together for three months. I was singing every day so that my voice would be in good shape. I enjoyed singing in Italian, English, and German, but when it came to the French language, I struggled. I found it difficult to pronounce and sing French words at the same time. In the French song I chose, one that I had sung while completing my bachelor's degree, I would always, without fail, forget the words that started the second verse. So I worked hard on this spot and got to the point that the words came to mind—and I could continue the song without stopping.

The day of the audition came, and I was a nervous wreck. I had been performing at church for more than three years, and I had many musical experiences to my credit, so why was I so nervous? I guessed that it was because this was college, and I hadn't performed at a college since the days of my bachelor's program.

I drove to the college with my accompanist, and we went into the recital hall. I was early, so a bathroom break was in order. In the restroom, I met (I found out later) one of the professors who would be listening to me. She was pleasant to me, and she left to go into the recital hall while I made final adjustments to my outfit. I went into the recital hall and sat down with my accompanist. Four professors came in, and it was time to begin.

My accompanist and I took our places at the piano and the stage respectively. I had four songs prepared, and they were to choose which song I was to sing. One of the professors asked me to sing the French song. Great. I was hoping and praying that I would remember verse two. I looked over at my accompanist, and we began. The beginning of the song went great. I sang energetically, and the professors all looked up at me and noticed. Then came the piano interlude, and then verse two. I drew a blank as usual, and we had to stop. The professors said that was okay and to continue. I went over to the music and looked at the words and started in again with verse two. I felt horrible. I was afraid that I had ruined my audition and would not be accepted into the program. I then had to sing my Italian piece, and it went well.

After I sang, I was asked to come down off the stage and talk to them. By the tone of their voices and the questions they asked, I could tell that I was accepted into the program. They didn't care if I forgot the words. They liked my voice, and I was in. I was so relieved.

The audition was in March of 2005, and I started classes in June. I was excited about it, but soon my excitement turned into dread and despair. I signed up for all the classes that were offered, not knowing that this was a bad idea. I had to get up at 5:30 in the morning, leave the house by 6:30 a.m., drive fifty minutes to the university, find a parking place, and get to class by 7:30 a.m. Classes went until five. I would arrive home by six. I had little time to do homework, eat supper, do chores around the house, and sleep. The classes were scheduled Monday through Thursday, with Fridays off. I recall collapsing on the couch on Thursday nights.

I was also having difficulty with online assignments that the music history professor was giving. I couldn't seem to download the articles for our reading assignments. I recall the first week of classes sitting in front of the computer and crying, ready to quit because of this. The problem was fixed only after I talked to others in my class and found the right path to the articles. I didn't quit, but I learned not to take so many classes the next summer.

When the classes were over that first summer, I was ready for a vacation—any vacation, anywhere. A couple of my single girlfriends had visited the Grand Canyon. After listening to their descriptions of their visit, I couldn't wait to go also. So at the end of July, Dan (he had outgrown *Danny* by then) and I took a plane ride west to Las Vegas. We had a layover in Minneapolis and arrived a good hour after we were supposed to be in Las Vegas. I had reserved a rental car online ahead of time, just as I had done with the hotel and the cabin at the canyon.

But when we arrived at the airport in Las Vegas later than expected, our rental car had been given to some basketball player. Apparently a basketball team had arrived there and taken all the mid-sized cars. I had to go to the next rental place, a more expensive one, and try to rent a car. Luckily, I had enough extra money to pay for it.

We took a shuttle bus to the car rental business, and I was given car keys and a number to a car and sent out to the parking lot to find it. My son and I located the car, but it had bird poop all over the outside of it, and it hadn't been cleaned inside. So we went back inside and told the employee what we had found. He went out and looked at it also. He agreed with me that the car wasn't ready to rent. So he took us to a fenced lot in the back of the business that was full of convertibles. Beautiful convertibles! Silver with black top convertibles!

The employee told me to pick any car I wanted to. I picked the closest one, signed the final papers, put the copy of the agreement in the glove box, and we hopped in the car. We followed directions toward the hotel I had reserved, but on the way we stopped to get gas. Once at the gas station, we put the top down. But we had to turn around and go back the way we had come. We could see Las Vegas Boulevard from the gas station and knew that we had made a wrong turn.

It was perfect weather. We drove from stoplight to stoplight on Las Vegas Boulevard, taking in the sights in our beautiful convertible. Each and every stoplight turned red on us, and sometimes we had to wait for a light two or three turns. But we didn't mind. We got to see the attractions of Las Vegas up close and personal. True, we didn't plan to go to any shows, but the buildings were gorgeous. We got to our hotel and settled in our room.

The next morning we ate at a luxurious breakfast bar in the hotel. With Dan being under the legal age, we chose not to play any slot machines or do any gambling or card playing. Our destination was the canyon. We already had a map and a plan to drive there, but I decided it would be a good idea to ask the desk clerk the shortest and best route to the canyon. He pushed a couple of buttons on a computer, and out popped a printed set of directions. It would take us about four hours to get there. We thanked him and left.

When we got to the convertible, we put the top down again, deciding to get some sun while we drove. But compared to the previous night's coolness, the day was hot and muggy. We couldn't take the heat for very long, so we pulled over and put the top back up and turned on the air. On the way to the canyon, we stopped and looked at Hoover Dam and Lake Mead and took some awesome pictures. We arrived at the canyon in time to eat and take a short hike before dark. The canyon was breathtaking. It was virtually indescribable. To appreciate the Grand Canyon's magnificence, one has to see it in person.

There was a storm that first night, and we almost got caught in it. But we found a shuttle bus stop and hopped on one. After we got on it, we weren't sure where to get off, it being our first night there. So we rode on it quite a while during the storm while the driver stopped and picked up other folks who were out in the storm. We were thankful to be dry on that bus. Lots of other folks were soaking wet.

On the second go-round on the bus route, we realized where our cabin was and got off. With the storm, the power was out in our cabin, along with the rest of the cabins at the canyon. There was a generator light in the hallway, but that was it. We had paid for an air-conditioned room but had to open the windows that first night. Our room was one of several in a large cabin. We had trees over our window so that we could open it some without any rain coming in. I did struggle a bit though, trying to open the window in the dark, not knowing how to operate the latches. The electricity came back on around five o'clock the next morning.

The next day, we listened to a lecture by a forest ranger, saw California condors, visited a gift shop, took a bunch of pictures, and went on a helicopter ride over the canyon. I took video footage of the canyon from the helicopter, and I still love to watch that video to this day. The view of the canyon was, again, breathtaking and indescribable. I was elated to be in the helicopter and sad when the ride was over. Dan enjoyed the ride, but he was not as excited as I was.

On the way to the helicopter ride, we had to leave the park. I had paid for a weeklong park pass, and we needed it to get back in the park after the helicopter ride. I thought that I had put it in a safe place in our room, but could not find it that morning. When we drove back to the park in the evening, the woman at the gate would not let us reenter, because she needed to see that park pass. I told her that I couldn't find it in our rush to get to our helicopter ride, and I showed her our cabin room keys to prove that we were staying there. She eyed the convertible and obviously did not believe that I was telling the truth. So I had to pay again to enter the park, but she mentioned that I could get a refund on the way out once I found my pass. After a thorough search back at the room, I found it in a pocket of my main suitcase. I was relieved. I would certainly ask for that refund.

On our third day at the canyon, we were to hike down into it. It was about a five-mile trip one way.

My son refused to get on the mules they had there, so we hiked. I had borrowed a pair of hiking boots from a friend who had already been to the canyon and had helped us to plan our trip. We started out at six in the morning on the trail that the mules take. It was a good five-feet wide and marked well.

We started out with jeans and long sleeves, but within an hour, we changed into our shorts and sleeveless tops at a public restroom. We had one backpack that we took turns carrying. In it we had water bottles and peanut cracker snacks. The path wove back and forth in a kind of zigzag while going down the side of the canyon. As we walked we had to step over mule droppings several times.

I stopped every so often to take pictures. The best pictures taken were looking back up the canyon and panoramic shots. I was excited and happy to be in one of God's creations. We saw many different rock formations, some foliage, and a couple of waterfalls, and we stopped at a couple of rest areas. We realized that it would be a long way back up the canyon, so we stopped at the Indian Gardens, which were located four miles down. We decided we had gone far enough. We rested a bit and ate our snack, which we shared with a pudgy, pushy squirrel that made the Indian Gardens his home.

On the trek back up the canyon, Dan had to carry the backpack. Every time I put it on my back, my steps got slower and heavier. He didn't complain too much. After we stopped at the rest area at the three-mile mark, I noticed that my left hiking boot was starting to fall apart. The rubber sole was coming loose. I had not packed another pair of shoes in the backpack, so we decided to keep going before it totally fell apart. Around the two-mile mark, the rubber sole came off, and only the material of the shoe was left on the bottom. I could feel the dirt and rocks on the trail. My foot didn't get too hot with the heat of the trail, though, which was a good thing. I had to stop more often while hiking back up the trail. I would last about two zigzags and have to sit down to rest. Fortunately, the stitching on the hiking boot held it together, and we made it up the canyon. The entire trek took most of the day, totaling about eight hours. Exhausted, we sat on the bench at the top of the trail and ate sandwiches from the vendor there. When we got back to our cabin, I took off the hiking boots, turned them over took a picture of them and then had to throw them away. I praised God for holding them together for me.

The next day I could hardly move. My legs ached so badly, all we did was rest and pack and do a little shopping. (My legs actually hurt for three days.) I bought a CD with Hopi Indian music on it. On the fourth morning of our stay at the canyon, after getting my money back for paying to get into the park a second time, we headed back toward Las Vegas. On the road leading out of the canyon, we listened to the Hopi CD, and I had few tears in my eyes. The music was gentle and appropriate as we watched the canyon disappearing behind us. The rest of the trip included high winds and storms.

We had a great visit, and I was sorry for it to end. We wanted to stop at the Hoover Dam, but with the bad weather, we took pictures from inside the car and kept going. We arrived in Las Vegas around rush hour and found the car rental garage in the nick of time before we had to pay for another day. We stayed at a cheaper, business-type of hotel that night, took a shuttle to the airport the next day, and had a direct flight to the airport one hour from our house. Upon arrival at the airport, we got our bags, located our car in the parking area, and drove home with a gorgeous sunset following us all the way home. What a beautiful ending to a beautifully exhausting trip.

2006:
Winking

B ack at home, it was business as usual: doing chores around the house and going back to work. Dan would be a senior that coming school year and was happy about it. He was a good student and never missed a day. At his high school, a student could waive one exam if they had perfect attendance for the year. Of course, his goal was to waive one of his exams. He went to school through sickness and health. The truth of the matter was that he struggled with tests, and this was his way to avoid his most difficult one. I was proud of him, because he was on the honor roll all the way through high school. We scheduled college visits, and he decided to attend my alma mater. I was thrilled. The visit and orientation process were fun and brought back many memories for me.

With my son soon to graduate from high school, I knew that I would be alone more of the time and the empty-nest syndrome would be weighing heavily on me. So I spent almost every night online viewing dating websites, signing up, putting my picture online, and "winking." On these dating websites, when people liked another person's profile, they would wink a hello to him or her. If the other person winked back, online communication occurred and then possibly an actual date. During the next couple of months, I had several dates, but there was no chemistry. Most of the time the men I winked at winked back right away, but there was one man who did not wink back. So I went out with whoever I could and got quite a bit of practice at dating.

A couple of months went by, and I needed a hysterectomy. In mid-November I had the operation, which went smoothly with a good recovery. But those hot flashes were terrible. Each time a hot flash started, I felt like I was having a heart attack. The doctor gave me some medicine to help, but it didn't help. I tried herbs and they helped but had difficult side effects. So, in the end I stopped taking anything and suffered.

With the six-week recovery, I was off work and didn't go back until January. It was rough just lying around, but I had no choice if I wanted to get better. I was still looking at online dating sites, but not going on many dates. Mostly I watched television, worked my puzzle books, and ate soup. Dan was very helpful while I recovered. He went to the store and helped around the house. By Christmas I was feeling better and getting around better than before.

One day, late in December, I was checking my online dating website and found that the man that I had winked at back in early October who did not wink back had now, out of the blue, winked at me. I was not impressed. Why did he wait so long? Well, he wrote me a long, drawn-out e-mail about how his mother had died and he had a lot to deal with. And then his dog died one week later. He had two deaths to deal with and all the sadness and funeral and house arrangements to contend with.

I was skeptical at first, but after reading his e-mail through a couple of more times, I believed he was telling the truth. So I e-mailed him back, giving my condolences and asking him if he wanted to meet me. He e-mailed back a yes. When dating online, it is always prudent to meet in a public place for the first date. I lived in a tiny town with no popular restaurants. He lived in a bigger town with several nice restaurants. So we chose a restaurant there. We were to meet there at six on December 29, 2006.

I arrived right on time and had to park in a side parking lot, since the restaurant was busy. I went and stood outside by the door of the restaurant per our agreement. I was there about a minute and saw an extremely tall, bald man frowning as he walked by in the front parking lot. He appeared to be looking for something or somebody. He was totally scary looking. It dawned on me that he was probably my date. Panic struck me, and my body reacted. I rose up on my toes, ready to sprint back to my car before he saw me. I was just about to sprint when God's voice spoke to me saying, "Selah," which means wait. I relaxed a little and shifted my weight back off my toes. My insides were in knots. What was I getting into?

He was walking back across the parking lot when he spotted me. There was no escape. He walked up to me and asked if I was his online date, and I said yes. We exchanged names. His name was Ty. We went in and were seated immediately. With the amount of people waiting, I was impressed. I found out later that they have a call-ahead plan so that, if you time it right, you can call ahead so many minutes and then arrive when you say, and be seated faster than just showing up at the restaurant.

So we went in and sat in a booth. And Ty talked, and talked, and talked. He did ask me a few questions, and I did get a few questions in myself, but mostly he talked. I did get to watch his expressions and mannerisms, and I laughed at the appropriate times. I recall liking the look of his face and arms and that he had a nice speaking voice.

We had a nice dinner and then went to a local coffee shop, where he found out that I didn't drink coffee, so we ordered hot chocolate. After finishing our hot chocolate, we took a drive around town and went by his house. He asked me if I wanted to come in and see his miniature orange tree, and I declined. On the drive back to the restaurant parking lot, I mentioned to him that if I didn't make plans for New Year's Eve, I would have to baby-sit. For many, many New Year's Eves, I had been home alone with my kids. We usually had fun, but after so many years, it had become boring. They were old enough now that I didn't need to baby-sit, but Jozie would usually ask me to watch her son when she went out.

I was tired of being with children on New Year's Eve. I wanted to be with adults. So I mentioned three different times in the car that I would have to baby-sit if I didn't have any plans. Ty took the hint and said he would call me and set up something for that night. I also received a phone call from Dan, who was at home on Christmas break and checking to see if I was all right. We were sitting in the car during this phone call, so Ty knew about it. I was a little embarrassed, but Ty thought it was nice that my son was checking on me.

When we arrived at my car, I was uncertain what I should do. We stood by my car and talked a bit more. While we were talking, a man suddenly appeared behind Ty. I panicked and prayed. God told me to kiss Ty, and I hesitated a second or two. Then I stood on my tiptoes and kissed him. (Ty is six feet tall, and I am only five foot two.) The man didn't leave, so I kissed Ty again. Ty was surprised at my actions, and I giggled a bit. I pointed out to Ty that there was a man behind him. Ty turned around and acknowledged the man.

The man looked at me and then at Ty and asked if he could borrow money to make a call. Ty said apologetically that he didn't have any cash on him. The man eyed both of us again and then turned and quickly walked away. I found out later that there had been reports of a man fitting his description mugging people in that parking lot. Maybe the mugger had a soft spot for lovers. Again God had protected me and who I was with at the time. After talking a bit more with Ty that night, I got in my car and drove home.

2007:
A New Year—
The Good and the Bad

I was humming to myself as I did chores around the house the next day. I was happy and I knew why. This man seemed genuinely interested in me. I hadn't exercised in weeks due to my operation, and I still parted my hair on the side and used my handy barrette. What did he see in me? I wasn't sure. He had a full-time job, a house, his own car, and a miniature orange tree, which was more than some of the jokers I had previously dated. I thought back on the date and remembered his arms—his strong forearms. I couldn't remember the color of his eyes, but I remembered his nice forearms.

I was trying to keep myself busy while I waited for his phone call. And I *was* waiting for his phone call. In my short, past dating experiences, I learned not to call the man. When I did try this, the relationship was over before it began. So I waited, and Ty called. I was so excited, but knew better than to show it over the phone. We talked a bit and Ty invited me over to his house for New Year's Eve. He wasn't a drinker and didn't want to be out on the roads that night. He was to pick me up, and I agreed to bring some snacks, board games, and one of my favorite music videos along.

He was right on time, but I was not quite ready. So I invited him into my living room while I went and put the final touches on my makeup and hair. When I came back to the living room, he mentioned that he liked my Christmas tree. I thanked him, and then we got in his car and headed for his house. Once there, we ate pizza and the snacks I had brought along. We watched a little television, and then I asked him to put in the music video that I had brought along. With the music video playing, I asked him if he wanted to dance, and he said yes. We were hesitant at first, but soon he was holding me close and looking in my eyes. No man I had ever dated looked at me the way Ty looked at me that night. I tried to keep looking into his eyes, but he was six feet tall. Talk about a crick in my neck! But, seriously, I liked the way he was looking at me. Then he reached down and kissed me. A soft, inviting kiss. I kissed him back, and we were soon sitting on the love seat he owned, making out. I had kissed other men, but not like this.

After a while we stopped kissing and watched the ball drop on television. We kissed again to welcome in the new year. I knew then that I wanted many more kisses with this man. We watched a little more television, and then I let Ty know I wasn't going to stay the night. So Ty, gentlemen that he was, took me home. I slept well that night, with visions of Ty in my head. (I know, too corny.)

On New Year's Day, I woke up and thought about Ty most of the day. I found myself humming again as I did chores around the house. I was happy and hoping deep down that this new relationship would last. From my reading on dating, I knew that it was important to get past the first two months of dating. If that was accomplished, the relationship had a good chance of survival. I was turning fifty that year, and I needed this relationship to work. Fifty, wow. I didn't feel fifty, or what I imagined a person should feel like at that age.

I was hoping that Ty would get to know me before hearing about all the problems with Jozie. And it just so happens that she showed up at my door that very day, New Year's Day, 2007. She had brought her daughter and son with her. I was surprised to see her, since she didn't call ahead or let me know what was going on with her. I welcomed them in, and Jozie sat down at the kitchen table. I got to hold Samantha, which was a blessing for me, since I hadn't seen them in a while. With my operation, I had not invited anyone over for Christmas, although I had gone to my family's gathering at my mom's house.

We talked a bit about nothing, and I noticed that she looked like she didn't feel so good. For a few minutes she didn't say anything. Then she told me that Samantha's dad hit her in the nose. I looked closer at her, and it didn't look like her nose was broken. So I gave her some acetaminophen for her headache and an icepack for her nose. I asked her why he would do that, and she said she didn't know. She had told him that she was leaving him and he went "off," whatever that means.

Right when I was trying to get to the bottom of the problem, Ty called. I picked up my phone and tried to remain calm. It was good to hear his voice. We talked a bit, and I let him know that I had a great time the night before. He agreed with me. He reminded me of the wonderful time that we had dancing and kissing. With Jozie in the room, I agreed with him, but I did not elaborate in great detail about our dancing and kissing. I needed to cut the phone conversation short, so I let Ty know that my daughter was there and in a bit of trouble, and I needed to help her. He said that he understood and that he would call me tomorrow. I said that would be great.

I got off the phone and asked Jozie if she wanted to file a police report. I thought she should. I was angry at Samantha's dad and worried about my daughter. I knew it was probably not the first time that he had gotten angry enough to hit her, so I asked. She said that it was the worst time but would not elaborate about what went on, probably to protect my feelings. So I pushed the issue of filing a police report right away, and she agreed to go.

We went to the city where she had been living, and she talked to a policeman while I watched the kids. I recall that it took at least an hour, and her son and I were running out of things to do. So he and I started throwing around my gloves. That is what I remember most about the trip: throwing around my gloves with my grandson.

When Jozie finally emerged from the other room with the policeman, she seemed calm, and it didn't look like she had cried too much. I hugged her, and we made our way home. Her things were at Samantha's dad's house, but we would have to get them another time. He was probably still hung over and in a bad mood. We decided to load up her things on a moving truck when we expected him to be at work.

Later that week, I helped her with this while he was at work. We had to do it quickly so as not to confront him at all. Within a couple of hours, we had loaded up all of her and her children's things into a moving truck and put them in my garage, which had been Dan's bedroom. Now we had three actual bedrooms, which was almost enough for all of us to live in. The garage was three-fourths bedroom and one-fourth storage room. Even with our shed in the backyard, I still needed room for tools and things.

Once Jozie had moved in with Samantha's dad, I had Dan move out of the garage and into the other actual bedroom to save on the electric bill. Now that Jozie was back, I left Dan in the house in his bedroom and put her and her kids in the garage/bedroom. So much for my electric bill. It was winter, and the space heater ran every day and night to keep the room warm for them.

Jozie slept all night and almost all day. Exhaustion consumed her. Depression was her middle name. I had to wake her up when Samantha cried. She left her television on all night, and who knows what her son was watching. Her bedroom was always a mess, with clothes and toys strewn everywhere. This went on for about a month. I dragged Jozie and her kids to church with me. I was still the choir director at my church, and it mattered to me that they were there. They went, but Jozie's heart was not in it. Years before, the last time she was with me, when her son was two years old and before she met Samantha's dad, we had a baptism ceremony for her son. It was nice. He was such a happy little guy, always smiling and curious. When I look at the pictures from that day, it reminds me of how innocent and happy he was.

I was still dating Ty and so happy with him. He rarely spent much time at my house. We usually went out, and on most weekends I packed an overnight bag and spent Saturday nights with him at his house. I had to get back to church for Sunday mornings to direct the choir, conduct the bell choir, and lead the praise songs.

Early in our dating, Ty attended one of our church services without telling me that he was coming there. I was thrilled and nervous that he was there. Later he said that he enjoyed the service and that I did a good job directing, even though the choir was small. Ty actually came to several services after that surprise visit, and we went to lunch afterward. We talked on the phone on Tuesdays and Thursdays after nine o'clock. He had a different cell phone plan than I did, so we used our minutes wisely. Since we would talk for a good two hours each time, we used the free time after nine o'clock. I remember sitting in my front enclosed patio room in a cushy, corner chair, and talking to him until the phone was so hot that I had to hold it away from my ear a little to continue talking to him. I was probably falling love then but didn't recognize it yet.

February arrived nastily cold and snowy, and Jozie moved out. She told me one day, and within a week she had moved in with her son's dad, who lived about one hour away. Okay, thanks for the notice. She had been in contact with her son's dad all along and didn't tell me. She was an adult, so I could not and should not tell her what to do. At least I didn't have to help her move this time. Her son's dad came and moved her out while I was at work. She told me years later that the rental truck broke down on the way there. Was she having fun yet?

I was glad that she moved out, but also concerned for her well-being. True, her son's dad had a job and an apartment. But could he handle a disabled child that was not his? Samantha had serious health issues and she was getting bigger. I was also skeptical that he would care for his son, since he hadn't called me or helped in any way after his son was born. True, he was only in high school then. But I expected him to try harder than he did to see his son. He didn't help pay for much of anything back then either, so I was surprised to find that he was willing to take care of everything now. Well, it was out of my hands. I had other, more fun and exciting people to focus on.

2007:
Valentine's Day Surprise

Ty told me he was taking me out to dinner for Valentine's Day to a "surprise" restaurant. I was so excited! He also took me shopping the weekend before the dinner to find something for me to wear. He waited patiently while I tried on dresses, and we picked out a red, knee-length one. He decided that I needed a purse and shoes to match, so we found those also. I felt so wonderfully young in the outfit. And if I do say so myself, it looked great on me. Who was this man, buying me clothes and taking me out to an expensive restaurant for our first Valentine's Day? He was certainly making an impression on me. This first Valentine's Day was so special that Ty likes to tell the story. So here is his version of our very first Valentine's Day date:

> 'I picked her up right on time as was my usual manner. We drove over an hour to the "surprise" location, which was a French bistro. I had made the reservations several

days before. I had gained her permission to celebrate Valentine's Day early due to the actual day falling in the middle of the week. It was a balmy fourteen below zero that evening. All I could think about was how cold her feet must have been in her new, red, open-toed shoes.

We arrived at our destination, and I noticed the look of delight on her face as she smiled warmly at me. We entered the restaurant, and they took our coats and seated us at our table. The waiter arrived with menus and water, and we took a while to decide what we wanted to eat. After ordering, I waited for her to do her usual visit to the ladies' room, but to my dismay she just sat there and drank her water. I wanted her to leave, because I had a surprise for her in my jacket pocket, and I wanted her to find it in front of her plate when she returned from the ladies' room. But she just sat there and would not leave.

We had been dating for six weeks, and I wanted this to be a very special evening. We talked and the minutes flew by, and I knew that soon the waiter would be back with our dinner. My plan was falling apart. My mind raced on what I should do next, and I became frustrated. I finally reached into my pocket and pulled out a small, velvet-covered black box and placed it on the table in front of her. I said, "This is for you."

The following moments I will never forget as long as I live. It was like watching a movie in slow motion. After I had placed the box in front of her, she looked up at me and her jaw dropped. Her eyes became big as saucers. She sat there looking horrified. The silence was deafening. Finally, my mind registered what she must be thinking. She thought I was proposing! I looked into her eyes and could tell that this was exactly what she was thinking. I finally said, "Just open it." Three times.

Her hands trembled as she opened the box. As she looked at the contents of the box, the color began to return to her face. She looked down and saw a beautiful pair of diamond earrings. Once she saw that it was not an engagement ring, she broke out into a nervous laughter that had other folks glancing our way. We both had a good laugh as she agreed with me that she had thought it was a ring. The waiter brought our food, and we both relaxed as we enjoyed our dinner.

After we ate, she did go to the ladies' room and put the earrings on. She wore them all the way home.'

Quite a nice story, don't you think? I was in love, and it felt wonderful. I tried to think back to my first marriage to see if I ever felt like this, and I couldn't recall a single night like it. Was my feeling of being as nasty as a cockroach starting to fade? Somewhat. Was Ty the man who could look past my past and see the real me?

I had not told him yet about my ex in any detail at all. That would come in time. We needed to get past the two-month mark. So, we exchanged e-mail addresses and Ty would write the most awesome love letters to me. Here is his first e-mail, written on Tuesday, February 13, 2007, with some added comments:

"My Darling,

I want to wish you a very happy Valentine's Day. How I wish I could be with you now. To hold you in my arms. To hug you and kiss you. To tell you how much you really mean to me. I still wonder if I'm dreaming sometimes. If I am, I hope that I never wake up. Being with you has been such a joy to me. Be it riding in the car together, snuggling, or attending church. I can only thank God Almighty that He let us be brought together.

And I thank you again for contacting me in the first place. How fortunate I am that you chose me. A woman like you who could have any man. [You're kidding, right?] Yet you picked me. I am humbled and blessed by your grace, your beauty, and your affection for me.

A woman like you completes me. You have it all, darling. The most beautiful green eyes that I have ever looked into. The sweetest, moistest lips I have ever kissed. The nicest hands I have ever held. The softest skin I have ever touched. The most loving arms that have ever embraced me. The most wonderful voice I have ever heard. I am so in love with you. You are my first, last date. All I want is you. All I need is you. [Sounds like a familiar song.] You are the woman I love and adore. You are the only woman I will ever need. I said I want to grow old with you, and I meant it. [And I am old.] Someday I will look into your eyes every night and tell you how much I love you. Someday I will hold you in my arms every night as we fall asleep together. Someday.

Please call me Wednesday evening after your business has been completed. I await and desire your call, O' beautiful and fair maiden. [Wow!] And it was such a pleasant surprise to hear from you today. You are so sweet to have been thinking about me and wondering if I was okay. Your love and affection for me have me dancing on air.

With love from me to you,
XXXXXXXXXXXXXXXXXXXXX
OOOOOOOOOOOOOOOOOOOO
Ty"

Wow! No other man had ever written me anything close to that. I was totally flattered and surprised and hoping that he really did mean what he said. I had heard of men who go off the deep end for a woman and then shortly after lose interest. So, plan A was to exercise every day and eat very little and keep kissing him on every date. And that is precisely what I did. I exercised daily, received love e-mails from Ty, and kept dating and kissing him.

We made it past the two-month period, and we searched for and attended a new church together. I had resigned my music minister position at the small church in my hometown so that I would have time with Ty and could get the rest that I needed, since my surgery had thrust menopausal hot flashes on me. Ty would call me twice a week, and then we had the weekends together.

Life around me seemed hazy and unimportant. All I wanted to do was be with Ty. There was very little news from Jozie. She seemed to be getting along okay with her son's dad. I visited them once or twice in the next few months. Dan was about to graduate from high school with honors.

During the month of April, Ty and I were sitting eating dinner at a nice restaurant one evening when I felt the urge to tell him what my ex had done to my daughter. We had been dating for almost four months now and I had been wanting to tell him but didn't quite know how or when to do it. The urge to tell him was so great, it seemed to overwhelm me. So, after we were done eating, I gently told him what had happened so many years ago. I tried my best not to cry, and I managed pretty well with only a few tears falling. Ty's reaction was calm, collected and kind. He expressed his sadness at the news and just sat there and listened to me. He did not leave or blame me for the unfortunate circumstances. I was surprised and happy for his reaction and relieved that he took it so well. Deep down I felt that cockroach fading more and more.

One of my girlfriends got married that June, and I got to thinking how nice it would be to be married to Ty. It was her second marriage, and she seemed so happy. She asked me to sing at her wedding, and my son was to play the extra music on his computer. I was happy to oblige. We arrived at her country church early and I practiced my song. While I was standing on the front platform talking with Ty and Dan, I stepped backwards a little and fell down a small ramp that was attached to the platform. I went down fast and hard. I heard one of the guest gasp. Ty came over and helped me up. As I stood up I felt a sharp pain shoot through my right ankle. As I tried to walk on it I was almost in tears. I did not tell the bride. I did not want to let her down. Someone else, though, told her because after about ten minutes she came and asked me how my ankle was. I lied to her that it was fine. I sang through the pain and during the reception my ankle started to feel better. My son almost managed to play all of the extra music at the right time and in the right order. He was doing a great job until the ceremony was finishing up. For my friend's exit music, he lined up the wrong song on his computer, started it, realized his mistake, and immediately adjusted it to the correct song. But my girlfriend and I noticed. I don't think that most other people noticed though. Still, it was a beautiful ceremony.

Another wonderful thing happened in June. A while back, on one of our weekends together, Ty had asked me what one thing I would like to do the most before I die. I had never been asked this before, so

I gave it some serious thought before answering. About a week later he asked me the same question, and I had my answer ready. I told him that I would like to swim with dolphins. So we planned a trip to Florida together for the end of June to do just that. It was Ty's usual vacation time, and I was off for the summer, so off to Florida we went.

It was a wonderful trip from start to finish. The only trouble spots were a little mix-up at the airport and driving through a rainstorm to a special restaurant where Ty wanted to eat some key-lime pie. We stayed at a hotel in Key Largo, played tennis every morning before breakfast, and then spent the days sightseeing. We ate at nice restaurants, ate lunch on the beach, watched the sunsets, and enjoyed the street performers at Key West.

I was scheduled to swim with the dolphins at a local dolphin training area on the third day of our vacation. Ty bought a package deal where I could swim with a sea lion and the dolphins. First I got in the enclosed area with the sea lion. The trainer had me put on my life vest, and the sea lion came up onto the platform to say hello and shake my hand. Then I got in the water and swam out a little way from the platform. The sea lion swam out to me and gave me a gentle, fuzzy kiss on the cheek. I was dreading it and wondering how it would feel, but I was pleasantly surprised. Ty took some great pictures of the event.

After that we went to the dolphin area, and a group of us entered the platform area. Ty stood over in the spectator area and videotaped the entire event. Dolphins are awesome creatures. They are sleek and powerful. I did not actually get to swim underwater with them. I could have done that, but I didn't feel that I was a strong enough swimmer. So I was above water, and the dolphins did tricks for me. I was able to pet them, and they talked to me.

One of their tricks was jumping over a plastic bar that I held out beside me. I got a close-up view of how powerful they really are. Two dolphins jumped over that bar and almost over my head. Their timing was perfect. I remember looking up at them in awe. Their final trick was to give me a short ride between them as I held onto their dorsal fins. I was instructed by the trainer to hold my arms out to each side. I wasn't sure when the dolphins would surface, but when they did, I was taken by surprise and held on for dear life. They swam with me holding on for about ten feet, and it was over way too soon.

One of the trainers took my picture, and I had a grin a mile wide. Usually they charge money for the pictures, but when Ty mentioned that it was my fiftieth birthday present to swim with the dolphins, they gave me the picture for free. What a nice gesture that was! We took the picture home and hung it on the wall in Ty's house. The dolphin experience was the highlight of the trip.

2009: A Simple Wedding and a Difficult Good-Bye

After we returned home, I was not looking forward to turning fifty in July. We had already celebrated Ty's fiftieth birthday. I felt old. But the small party with my family was nice. I received the usual items labeled with the number fifty. In August, it was back to school, packing my son off to college, singing at church, and finishing my master's project so I could graduate in May. I was a busy lady for sure.

Dating Ty was fun, and we grew even closer. We kept our usual pattern of calling on Tuesdays and Thursdays and weekends together. And we went to church together on Sundays. Life was good. Christmas rolled around, and not only did I decorate my house, but I also helped Ty put up his Christmas tree. He had a fireplace at his house, and we had many wonderful nights cozying up near it.

We shared our second New Year's Eve together, and although it was nice, it wasn't as romantic as the first one. Let's just say I wasn't so caught up in the moment as I had been the year before. And while I'm on the subject, yes, we were doing it. We were having sex. And it was wonderful sex. The best I've ever had! I was in love—loving Ty and loving the way I felt.

I wish I had a cute, romantic story to tell about how he proposed to me, but I don't. On January 6, 2008, Ty and I had steamy sex, and he got down on his naked knees beside the bed and proposed to me. I accepted. We kissed, and we have been together ever since. Oh, we have had our disagreements and all-out fights, but we made a commitment to each other, we love each other very much, and we truly intend to grow old together. Really old.

We went to a jewelry store later that week, and I got to pick out my engagement ring. I wore it all the time and showed it to everyone who cared enough to notice. That old cockroach feeling was shrinking more and more.

The next few months were happy and busy. I finished my master's project and we attended the graduation ceremony in May. During the ceremony on the large football field, while diplomas are being handed out, I was thrilled to be in line to shake the university president's hand. Though the ceremony was long and the day was hot, Ty and my family were there with me, supporting my success.

June rolled around, and school was out. My son was home for the summer and working at his summer job. Jozie was doing fine, living with her son's dad. Then Ty asked me to move in with him. It was more economically sound to be paying one mortgage instead of two. He and I had also been discussing when and how to get married. Sometimes he suggested that we elope, and I kept insisting that my family should be present at a ceremony. We wanted a simple, inexpensive, nice wedding. So, through all the discussions, we decided to live together in Ty's house, which was bigger than mine, to let Jozie and her family move into my old house, and to get married the following spring.

The moves went fine but were a lot of work. It was an exciting time for me. Planning a future together with Ty was a dream come true. I had always wanted to be married, have a family, and grow old with someone. All three wishes were being fulfilled for me. I had been a single mom for many years, but through it all, God was with me.

After the moves, I made a master list of what we needed for the wedding, and each month I would buy something on that list. Some of my family members had experience in certain areas that helped us to save a bundle on wedding expenses: My older sister baked our heart-shaped, white wedding cake with red roses on it. We rented the tuxes from my sister-in-law. My brother took professional pictures during the ceremony. My brother-in-law videotaped the wedding. My sister-in-law also lent us the maid of honor's dress for nothing. And one of my nephew's played our selection of CD's for the ceremony and the reception.

I went dress shopping with my daughter and found one half-price at one of the best wedding shops around. It was only the second dress I tried on. I got some surprised looks from other people at the shop. I was the oldest bride there. Even the sales clerk was smirking a bit when I said that I was the bride and not my daughter. But, I didn't care. I was happy, and no one was going to ruin it for me.

My little sister helped me to sew twenty-seven (three rows of nine) small red roses on the train of my dress to match the red roses around the gazebo in the park where we married. The gazebo was in the middle of a large rose garden with every color imaginable and red roses right next to it. It was a beautiful setting for a wedding.

The months passed quickly, with all the planning and exercising and dieting and tanning that I had to do. I made my own invitations with the help of my computer. I made personal fans with our picture on them for people to hold if the day was warm (which it was). I did not ask for gifts, but did ask for food donations for the local food pantry. We ended up with a couple of boxes to donate.

Our wedding day, June 27, 2009, finally arrived, and all was ready. We had rented white outdoor chairs, bought a white runner to walk on, and set up a white canopy for the reception. We dressed in a rented house adjacent to the rose garden. Dan was to walk me down the aisle, and Jozie was the maid of honor. My grandson was the ring bearer, and a pastor that I had worked with years before performed the ceremony.

Everything was set, and the ceremony began. My little sister was there to help straighten my gown and cue me to start down the aisle. The pastor, Ty, and my grandson had gone first. I leaned on Dan's arm and started down the aisle toward the gazebo. I looked at Ty, and with each step closer to him, my heart warmed. As he looked at me, too, his eyes misted, and he shed a few tears. Wow! I had heard that some men do this, but I never expected my strong, muscular Ty to be so moved.

I paused for my brother to take a picture, smiled at the people standing on either side of me, and walked up the steps of the gazebo. I remember hearing a few gasps when my rose-decorated train came into view. We exchanged vows (Ty did some prayerful talking, and I sang a couple phrases of a French love song to him) and exchanged rings. The pastor prayed over us, and we became husband and wife.

I had wanted to dance on the way back down the aisle, but my dress and long train made that impossible. So I did a couple of small, joyous wiggles to the upbeat recessional music in the gazebo before we headed back down the aisle. The reception was next to the house where we had gotten dressed. We held our receiving line under the shade of a tree, then cut the cake, and then danced under the canopy set up beside the house.

All in all it was a lovely affair and a beautiful setting. The weather was warm, but nice. My daughter caught the bouquet. And I showed my ring to all my girlfriends. Ty and I posed for a few more pictures, and the wedding was over. The whole affair had lasted about four hours.

I changed out of my dress, we cleaned up the house; the rental place came and picked up the chairs and canopy; the tuxes were sent home with my sister-in-law; and we went out to eat. I had only eaten one meatball and one strawberry from the reception, so I was quite hungry.

For our honeymoon, we drove out west for a week, stayed in a cabin, and visited major landmarks. We fed prairie dogs, watched buffalo grazing, enjoyed seeing baby bears at play, petted young kangaroos, and were awed by a large double rainbow on the way home. We visited Wild West towns, ate at the best restaurants, and enjoyed buffalo burgers for the first time. Our cabin was so remote that we did not have any cell phone reception. Even though we asked for no gifts at our wedding, we did receive a couple of restaurant gift cards that we used during our stay.

When we got home, it was back to normal life and taking care of business. Dan had watched the house for us by watering the plants, getting the mail out of the mailbox, and making sure that the house was locked up at night. Jozie seemed to be doing fine while living at my old house. We did, however lower her rent to help her with her finances.

She and I had some lengthy discussions about her childhood, how she felt about it, and if she would ever want to press charges against her dad. She ended up deciding against it. We also discussed her need to confront him and tell him how she felt. She did want to meet with him, so I got busy and e-mailed him. (We had exchanged e-mails long before.)

We decided to meet him at a public place, which ended up being the university where her dad and I had both attended and met. Dan was attending the same university, so he was included in the meeting. We set the meeting up for the fall of 2010 on a Saturday.

We arrived at the university, picked up Dan, and found a parking space near the prearranged meeting spot. We were meeting in an outdoor eating café; I wanted an easy getaway, if needed. I wore one of my ball caps, thinking that I would appear more sporty and stronger (in mind only). I hadn't seen or talked to my ex since that Halloween pumpkin cutting visit back in 2000. I was somewhat fearful, but I knew that Jozie needed to do this. And I hoped that my ex would admit what he did, so there could be healing on all sides.

We arrived on time, and my ex was already there. My heart skipped a bit when I saw him, and fear started to creep into my mind. But he was pleasant and smiled a bit as we walked over to him, so I relaxed a little. We said our hellos, and the usual questions were asked. Then we sat down at a table, and my ex started reminiscing about when we had attended the university together. I steered the conversation back to the present day. I also showed him my wedding ring, letting him know I was married. He congratulated me. We talked some more about Dan's college life.

Jozie hadn't said two words the entire time. I was running out of things to say, so I nudged Jozie to say what she came there to say. I had encouraged her to write it down, take it with her, and read it. So she pulled her paper out of her pocket and read this to him:

"I can no longer let you control my life. I need to be free of you. What you did to me was inexcusable. I was your daughter. You were supposed to protect me, love me, be there for me and you hurt me in the worst way possible. You have broken my trust. You left me scared and feeling empty, and I have been stuck in a dark place all these years. But I am here to leave it with you. I can no longer be the five-year-old girl who is hurt and feels helpless. I can no longer let your actions dictate my life. I have hated you with every fiber of my being. I can't carry that with me anymore. So I am leaving, knowing that you won't get to ever know me or Dan or your grandchildren, and you are alone. And I have people who love me."

There was dead silence for as long as it took my ex to breathe in. Then he said to me, "Let's talk," as he stood up from the table. Dan took Jozie's little lap dog from her, and she hightailed it indoors to the nearest restroom. My ex and I took a walk in the other direction from the table. He adamantly denied any wrongdoing, pointing out that he had tested negative in that STD test so many years before. I told him that I had proof from other sources that he did do it. We argued back and forth as I stood up for my daughter. I said that if he wanted to carry this denial to his grave, so be it.

After a short walk and a circular conversation, we stopped and looked hard at each other. He asked me what Jozie wanted. I said that an apology was needed. When Jozie came back outside to the table, he did apologize to her for a few things. He said that he was sorry for leaving her alone and not being there for her. He apologized for not keeping in contact with us. Then he said a curt good-bye and walked away.

I walked over to Jozie, hugged her, and told her how brave she was. I asked her where her paper that she read from was, and she said that she had thrown it away. She and I walked back into that building and retrieved it from the trash can just outside the restroom. I kept that paper, because I had already started this book and wanted to include it. We stood there for a while gathering ourselves, then headed home, leaving Dan to his schooling.

Final Thoughts

S o, there has been no apology, no admittance, and no actual closure. I still get angry whenever I think about what my ex did. What a tragedy for everyone involved in this terrible, unspeakable act. I chose to believe my daughter when she told me about the molestation. I chose to make sure that it didn't happen again. But my daughter has suffered for many years. I can tell because of her life choices. She has had two illegitimate children by two different fathers and is now pregnant by yet another man. I know that she just wants someone to love her. She did not have a proper father figure to show her what to look for in a man.

I have tried to speak to her about this, but all my talking falls on deaf ears. All she has ever needed to do is to look to God to find the perfect father, but to my knowledge, she has yet to do this. It breaks my heart that I cannot be the happy grandmother. It breaks my heart that she has children out of wedlock, which makes it more difficult to rejoice and celebrate each birth. It breaks my heart each time

I think back to all of it and wish that I had done things differently.

I love my children, but I do think back to the day of my first wedding and wonder why I went through with it. Pride. It must have been pride. Maybe I also needed to save face. I don't know for sure. I know now that God was trying to warn me, but I was so confused. I was young and unsure of myself and my decisions. Because of my selfish pride, I have suffered for almost a lifetime. My children are damaged, I have had an isolated, lonely life, and the consequences are still playing out.

My anger consumed me for many years. Anxiety attacks used to be commonplace. I was angry at the world and didn't care if I showed it. My poor children had to grow up with this lonely, angry mother who did love them but wasn't very pleasant to be around. I had to make all the decisions, and I thought that I had to make sure they had everything they needed. I worked too many jobs, wasn't home enough, and when I was home, I was exhausted. More pride shining through.

But I cannot go back and change things. And I cannot keep looking back and apologizing and wishing I had done things differently. I can only look to God for guidance and reassurance that He has and will always be with me. In every situation, in every minute of every day, God was there. I needed only to stop, listen, and recognize His presence. This, of course, is not easy to do. It goes against human nature to let someone else be in charge. More pride, I guess.

But as I have looked back at my life to write this book, I see that it has been an awesome journey. True, my tears have flowed time and time again, just as they flowed when I was on my knees at many church altar calls through my single-parent years. But I have been able to see and recognize God being there, even when I felt the sorrow and loneliness overwhelming me. God was there protecting me from my ex and his family when they tried to take Jozie. God has been with me through everything. I only needed to let go and trust Him. Just like the old hymn says, "Through it all, through it all, I've learned to trust in Jesus, I've learned to trust in God..."

There have been many nights when I have asked God for guidance and opened my Bible. By reading the words He gave me, I have gained insight into what I was supposed to do. My journey has given me sorrow, but it has also given me more patience, more compassion, more understanding, and more love for others. My selfish pride has diminished some, and I have received many blessings.

One wonderful blessing is Ty, whose presence in my life is one of God's gracious gifts. Ty was an unexpected blessing because, after so many years of being alone and trying online dating for three years, I had almost given up on meeting my special someone. But God knows all things and provides in His timing. I thank God daily for His gift of Ty. We love each other, and even through our differences of opinion, we know our love will last for an eternity.

Looking back on my life, I know that I never gave up hope for a better future. To this day I still feel some anger toward my ex, but mostly I just feel sadness for my daughter, my son, and myself. Sadness for all the damaged children out there who are suffering in the same way, and sadness for the poor souls damaging the children. What a vicious cycle!

But I do believe that God wants us to be overcomers. There certainly is sin in the world that we have to overcome. We were born into sin; we make all kinds of mistakes and bad decisions. When bad things happen, God can and will open a path for us to take. No matter what other people do to us, we can overcome and go on with our lives.

God helped me to overcome my past by sending the Holy Spirit and lifting my depression. He also helps me every day as I pray and ask Him to lead me. For a while, I thought it was Ty who helped me to no longer feel like a cockroach, but I was wrong. God was the one.

God has given me courage and hope ever since I was born again. God gave me the courage to call my ex on the phone and tell him that I forgive him. God has helped me to claim "Cockroach no more!" True, Ty is my special someone, but God is my Abba, my Father, my Adonai who cares for me daily as I look to Him for everything.

About the Author

J eannie LaVerne was raised in a small town. Her story shows how one can overcome personal devastation with God's guidance.